MILLENNIUM

MILLENNIUM

Peace, Promises, and the Day They Take Our Money Away

TEXE MARRS

LTP Living Truth Publishers
8103 Shiloh Court • Austin, Texas 78745

About the Cover: Art for the cover of *Millennium* is from the painting *Beata Beatrix* (1870), by Dante Gabriel Rossetti. The radiant, red bird, with halo and bearing a poppy flower, represents arrival of the messenger of death amidst sudden spiritual transformation.

Second Printing

Millennium Copyright © 1990 by Texe Marrs. Published by Living Truth Publishers, a division of Living Truth Ministries, 8103 Shiloh Court, Austin, Texas 78745.

Scripture quotations are from the King James Version of The Holy Bible.

Cover design: Texe Marrs
Graphics and technical assistance: Sandra Schappert

Printed in the United States of America

Library of Congress Catalog Card Number 90-61633

ISBN 0-9620086-5-6

ACKNOWLEDGEMENTS

So many have assisted me in the production of this book, and I am grateful to each and every one who has generously given of their time and talent. I am especially appreciative of the outstanding work of Sandra Schappert whose superior skills, advice, and assistance in the areas of cover design, art, graphics, formatting and layout were invaluable. Lori Spurger, my assistant and secretary, did an excellent job and demonstrated a high degree of professionalism and team spirit to insure timely, quality production of the finished book.

To the other members of my staff, especially Beckie King and Ken Greene, Jr., and to the many who have written to encourage me and have prayed for me, I also give my sincere, heartfelt thanks. How God has blessed me with people who care!

I cannot even begin to express my gratitude to my wife, Wanda. Her support has made a tremendous difference in my life. Without her this book would not have been possible.

T A B L E   O F

Contents

INTRODUCTION

There is in the world today a secretive group of powerful men who are in every respect *conspirators*. Ruthless and determined, these men are utterly consumed by their lust for power and control and obsessed with an intensely passionate greed for money. I call these men *The Lords of Money*, or simply, *The Order*.

In *Millennium* I unmask the men of The Order, shine heavenly light on their ungodly activities, and expose the monstrous and cruel *conspiracy* which these men have, up to now, so masterfully orchestrated.

We are told in I Timothy 6:10 that "the love of money is the root of all evil." The men of The Order seek money not for its own sake but because of the power and influence that the *possession of money* allows them to wield. To them, money is a tool and a weapon. It buys influence within elitist circles, insures cooperation of reluctant officials, and--when necessary--strangles opposition.

The super-rich of The Order operate unsuspected in America, Canada, Europe, South America, Japan, and in practically every other nation on earth. Their combined wealth is mind-boggling. The members of The Order hold vast stores of currency, gold, and real estate. They control the largest banks on earth and supervise gigantic corporate empires spread across America and the globe. Still, their greedy appetites continue to be insatiable.

It is said that absolute power corrupts absolutely, and these evil men are, without question, *supremely and absolutely corrupt.* To get their way, they will stop at nothing, and *the financial destruction of America is now their fondest goal.*

A Hidden Power

The Order is the hidden power behind almost every decision made today by governments. Its elitist members hold in their invisible hands the incredible power to financially bring America to its knees and to plunge our nation into a bloody war of unbelievable magnitude. Indeed, these astonishing events lie just ahead on their well-established agenda to seize dominion and authority.

The influence of The Order in our everyday lives is staggering. Its loyal agents now hold positions in the highest levels of government and industry. Some are presidents or prime ministers of major nation-states; others exercise authority in the U.S. Congress and European parliaments. They serve as chairmen of huge megabanks and sit on the boards of Fortune 500 corporations. Not a few are members of European royalty, whose names, in *Millennium,* may surprise and startle you.

A number of top economists, TV executives, and newspaper journalists do the bidding of The Order. Their role in molding public opinion on important financial, religious, and political matters is deemed crucial to the objectives set forth by the elitist Lords of Money who seek a One World Order and Religion.

Regrettably, the super-rich world leaders who make up the conspiracy exposed in this book are now on the very threshold of succeeding beyond their wildest dreams. The stage has been set. Though they promise us a shining new millennium of unparalleled peace and prosperity, the awful truth will very soon be unveiled. *The day is almost here when they will take our money away.*

On that momentous day, they will set in motion their insidious yet ingeniously brilliant scheme to convince you and me--and peoples everywhere--to fall in line behind the great *World Leader* now in the wings. This is the man, one of their own, whom The Order has already chosen to lead us into what they claim will be a perfectly ordered, blissful *Seventh Millennium.*

But the Lords of Money cannot get what they want without first taking from you and me. Therefore, a global economic holocaust is on the way. It is virtually assured that a planned economic cataclysm will take place sometime in the decade of the 1990s, and quite possibly by 1993. Expect emotional outbursts, unbridled panic and an atmosphere of fear to mushroom as economic chaos looms and America is locked tightly in a financial, political, and military vise.

Though our banks and savings and loans are already going broke and closing their doors at an alarming pace, we will be haunted by the specter of even more banks and savings and loans failing in the days ahead. Wall Street will reel as the stock market crashes, and anger will erupt when the realization hits the American people that *their dollars are no longer legal tender* and that the *New Money* is to be issued by the few megabanks that are left.

A Fourth Reich and A New Rome?

The massive conspiracy that now confronts us is not entirely new. Its fascinating but stagnant roots lie in ancient Babylon, Greece, and Rome. Today, Bible prophecy is being fulfilled in a tremendous way as a United States of Europe emerges and a strong and assertive, united Germany fulfills its destiny of becoming the leader of a revived Roman Empire.

Will a united Germany--already an economic power-house with its mighty currency, the mark--spawn a new Hitler and a *Fourth Reich of the wealthy?* Will this Fourth Reich then become the *New Rome?* Are these, indeed, the last days?

In *Millennium* I provide the startling--and disturbing--answers to these awesome questions. The determined men who conspire behind the scenes today do in fact seek to restore the glories of ancient Rome. Moreover, they fully intend to complete the heinous mission which Hitler first set out to accomplish.

The members of The Order are followers of the *secret doctrine*, a mysterious body of occultic beliefs which, they believe, has endowed them with mystical vision and unparalleled supernatural powers. Confident in their purpose and in their expectation of success, the members of The Order claim to be extraordinary superbeings, chosen vanguards of a new race of Aquarian god-men who will reign over lesser races in the glittering millennium just ahead.

As such, they view the Bible as so much garbage and true Christians as ignorant and unsophisticated members of a lower-caste spiritual order. To them, we are an inferior species fit only for servitude and slavery . . . or worse.

The perversely decadent members of the exalted group I call *The Order* also assert that the people of the United States are a tainted, *mongrel race.* They claim this is so because of America's intermixing and intermarriage of so many ethnic groups and nationalities. Indeed, in *Millennium* I quote one of their leaders--*the head of the world's largest and richest corporation*--who arrogantly boasts that his is *"a race of completely pure blood, not a mongrelized race as in the United States."*

The Present Danger

America is passing through a dangerous period of severe economic decline. *Millennium* documents that our nation is *now owned by foreigners.* We have been forced to sell to outsiders the greatest treasures in America, and *this is a profoundly prophetic event.* Our president and congress are now under the yoke of foreign creditors, and they have little or no power to stop the rising tide of evil that now confronts us.

Who, then, can stop the evil plot--now far advanced-- of the elitist conspirators who so despise America and true Christianity? The answer is clear: God alone can do so. *And in His timing He will.*

This is why, although I hurt for the lost and the deceived, I am neither frightened nor dismayed over what is happening in today's world. Nor am I anxious over tomorrow's future. Truly, "Greater is He that is in you than he that is in the world" (I John 4:4).

The Lords of Money may scheme and plot to bring in their twisted One World Order. They may sincerely--but mistakenly--believe that their will shall be done by the time the Seventh Millennium of man dawns on planet earth. But it is God's plan that prevails. He promised us a coming, magnificent *Millennial Kingdom* that will last for a thousand years. And He will preside over it as our King and Lord! That is our Blessed Hope--and it is an ever present reality.

Even more fantastically breathtaking, the coming Millennium of Christ and His saints will be followed by a new heaven and a new earth that will endure for an eternity.

The plans of The Order are therefore puny indeed. Assured victory belongs to God. *Even so, come quickly, Lord Jesus!*

Texe Marrs
Austin, Texas

PART ONE

Unmasking the Lords of Money

ONE

The Day They Take
Our Money Away

For the love of money is the root of all evil...
(I Timothy 6:10)

*The Illuminati have ever led the race forward; the
knowers, mystics, and saints have ever revealed to us
the height of racial and individual possibilities.*
Alice Bailey
From Bethlehem to Calvary

A day is coming that will shake the world.
On that monumental day, fear and panic
will reign and people's hearts will fail
them. Some men and women will literally go out of their
minds; others will seek to escape by taking the ultimate
step: suicide. *All this will happen on the day they take our
money away.*

There is in existence today a secretive group of
ruthless men who have set out to control the world.
Moreover, they are on the very threshold of doing so.
These are the men who plot to take our money away and
replace it with empty promises and deceitful lies.
Endowed with great supernatural powers, they have the
consummate ability to instill fear and dread in their
opponents. Anyone who gets in their way or who

challenges their Plan becomes their enemy, and all enemies are eventually crushed.

Obsessed with greed and consumed with lust for money and power, this elite group of determined men believe that the key to their success will be their takeover of the world's money systems. To gain the willing acceptance of the masses for their ingenius scheme, they present to the unwary a masterful propaganda campaign. This campaign would suggest to us that instead of judgment, planet earth is about to enter a glittering *new millennium* of unparalleled peace and prosperity. In reality, we are all about to enter a brief, incredible era of dictatorial control and malevolence, a stunning period when peoples everywhere will cry out in their misery and despair.

The men of whom I speak may quite correctly be called members of a *conspiracy*, for they plot their goals jointly and in private, concealed behind a darkened veil of secrecy and intrigue. Because they are seducers of the truth who must hide their true identity, the top leadership--the core inner circle--of this conspiracy is often referred to in awe-inspiring tones by lower-level initiates who use such deceptive titles as:

The Masters of Wisdom	*The Lords of Compassion*
The Society of Illumined Minds	*Crusaders of the Green Cross*
The World Mind	*The Brain Trust*
The New Group of World Servers	*Torch Bearers*
The Masters of Wisdom	*Wise Men*
The Council of Masters	*The Council of All Beings*
The Order of One	*The Secret Brotherhood*
The Invisible Order	*Guardians of the Grail*
The Custodians of The Plan	*Great White Brotherhood*

I choose to call these men, with much justification, the *Lords of Money,* or simply *The Order.*

Unmasking the Conspirators

Having meticulously researched the inner workings of this hidden group of conspirators for some years, I find it remarkable that no one, before now, has been able to discover the identities of the men who comprise the higher echelons of The Order. In *Millennium* I will not only name some of the top conspirators, I will also unmask their hideous plans and expose many of their best concealed secrets.

I believe it is time we uncover the despicable operations of The Order. The stakes are far too high for us to remain silent. These ruthless men may well decide to lash out and seek to destroy me in anger and vengeance that their evil schemes are made transparent. True, that possibility exists. But though I am not unaware of the power and influence wielded by The Order, I am not afraid of what these men can do. My trust and faith is in God, and my life and care are in His hands:

> For whatsoever is born of God overcometh the world: and this is the victory that overcometh the world, even our faith (I John 5:4).

The Conspiracy of the Lords of Money

Our Bible clearly tells us that in the last days there will in fact be a veiled conspiracy of staggering proportions. This conspiracy is to culminate in the rise to power of the Antichrist, a political ruler of tremendous demonic strength. Power will "be given unto him to make war with the saints, and overcome them" (Revelation 13:7). Indeed, power is "given him over all kindreds, and tongues, and nations. And all that dwell upon the earth shall worship him, whose names are not written in the book of life of

the Lamb slain from the foundation of the world"
(Revelation 13:7, 8).

As you can see, we are warned in Revelation that all
the world shall worship this man. Now any criminal lawyer
will tell you that *just two or more people* who collude
together to commit an illegal act constitute the legal
definition of a "conspiracy." But here we see an instance
in which *all the world* colludes together, and *all peoples*
allow themselves to be manipulated and controlled by this
great conspiratorial world ruler.

Moreover, in II Thessalonians 2 we find Paul's
poignant prophecy that *in the last days*, just before Jesus'
second coming, *all the world* shall come under a delusion
so strong and so hypnotically compelling that *all* will
believe "the Lie" of the Antichrist... and be damned.

Today, The Order is readying its chosen leader for his
future dramatic role at the pinnacle of world power. Soon,
I am convinced, startling events will occur to propel this
man of destiny to international prominence and acclaim.
He will burst forth on the scene and be handed the reigns
of world power at a desperate time of peril and crisis for
humanity. And he alone will seem to have the solutions to
all our stupendous problems. He will appear to be the
only leader able to quell the crisis and restore peace and
prosperity.

The Real Millennium

The global conspiracy of the Lords of Money will succeed
for a time--until the end of this age when Jesus Himself
returns and does away with the schemes and connivings of
these evil men and their demonic overlords. Then, the
real millennium will be inaugurated and a bright new day
will shine forth for mankind.

Thus, it should be understood that although The

Order and its hand-picked leader succeed for a brief season, God is certainly in control of what is happening here on planet earth. In essence, he has turned these wicked men over to a reprobate mind because of their rebellion. They are sealed for destruction and their destiny is bleak. Indeed, their will is not their own "For God hath put in their hearts to fulfill His will, and to agree, and give their kingdom unto the beast until the words of God shall be fulfilled" (Revelation 17:17).

We see, then, that while the adversary has a Plan which now appears temporarily to be going smoothly, God has a *Greater Plan*, the culmination of which will be the victorious coming of our Lord Jesus Christ (Revelation 19:11-21).

The ungodly men of The Order have in mind for us a seventh millennium in which a superior race of god-men will take charge and guide the planet into a Golden Age of pleasure, selfishness, immorality, and gross materialism. Of course, according to the insidious but cleverly deceitful doctrine of The Order, only a few will be fit to thrive and rule during this Golden Age. The vast majority are misfits, ignorant and unworthy of divinity. They will be destroyed or else reduced to serf status. They are of a lower caste. Christians and Jews are the two primary groups that have been categorized by The Order as misfits and placed into the serf class.

What Do The Conspirators Hope to Achieve?

As I have stated, the vain men who comprise The Order realize that *he who controls the world's money controls the world.* Absolute control over all the world's money yields absolute power, and these men are absolutely corrupt. Being totally corrupt, decadent, and immoral, they will stop at nothing to gain their objectives.

Currently, their Plan calls for the crushing of America by means of a *great economic depression* that will dwarf the crash of 1929 and the 30s. Amidst the ensuing financial panic and the wreckage and carnage of this destruction, the elite men who make up The Order intend to issue a world currency. I refer to it in this book simply as the "New Money."

Following this takeover of the world's financial institutions, their goal is the establishment of a One World Political Order and a New Age World Religion. The Supreme Leader of The Order, the new fuhrer, will be at the helm of this colossal new global enterprise. In effect, he will preside over a *New Rome* and a new *Fourth Reich* of the super-rich.

Despisers of America

The top members of The Order do not love America. Nor are they imbued with the patriotic yearnings and heart-stirring motives typical of any good American citizen. No, their loyalty is to themselves ... and to The Order. Though many are U.S. citizens and some even occupy political and other offices and positions of great responsibility, they freely violate the public trust for their own greedy interests and to fulfill the work assigned them by The Order.

Seeing themselves as a superior race, they believe it is their destiny to lead all of humanity lock-step into a *global order* free of patriotism and nationalistic sentiment. As one of their own leaders describes it, their role is to further the causes of a *New Age* ... for a new breed of exalted, divine human beings--*Solar Man.*

Will The Conspiracy Succeed?

Will The Order succeed in its objectives? Will the Lords of Money be able to establish the New Rome, complete with a modern-day Caesar and a universal religion?

Before we too hastily say no, concluding that such a scheme by conspirators could never possibly succeed, we should first seek wisdom from God's Word. The fact is, we know that *someday* such a conspiracy *will* succeed. Revelation 13:7-8 describes a day when a small group of blasphemous men ascend to the very threshold of total world power. They will rule "over all kindreds, and tongues, and nations" (Revelation 13:7).

Moreover, according to God's Word, the evil man who leads this successful conspiracy will prove so dynamically popular and charismatic that he will win over the masses by widespread, virtually universal acclaim and consensus (Revelation 13:12; Daniel 11:21). And he will get his greedy way about money, too, for in Daniel 11:39-43 we read that "he shall have power over the treasures of silver and gold" and will "divide the land."

The frightening truth is that Bible prophecy depicts a coming period when a demonically led conspiracy will so totally control the earth "that no man might buy or sell, save he that had the mark, or the name of the beast, or the number of his name" (Revelation 13:17).

Who is the "beast?" Revelation 13:18 identifies him as the head of the world conspiracy, a man loved by people everywhere, and a man with a number. That number will be 666.

So the question is not *will there be a conspiracy?*, but *when will God, in His wisdom and timing, permit a power- and money-driven conspiracy to succeed?* Clearly, as this book will amply demonstrate, Satan has inspired a unique cartel of evil men who are even now far advanced in their outrageous but astonishingly brilliant scheme to take over this planet.

It has taken the Adversary thousands of years and many dress rehearsals to get this far, and he has failed many times in the past. For example, we are told in II Thessalonians 2 that even in the days of the early church, the "mystery of iniquity" was already at work but was being hindered by heavenly powers from achieving its ultimate goals. Today, if it be God's will, the mystery of iniquity will finally achieve its malignant aims. The conspiracy of the super-rich will soon be rewarded for its perseverance and its unrelenting and boundless ambition.

The Conspiracy That Rages

The evidence of a conspiracy at large in the world today is so massive and compelling that one would have to be an utter fool not to recognize its existence. One would also have to deny the Word of God.

How amusing it is when people sometimes challenge me and say, "Come on, Texe... a *conspiracy*?" "Why, that could never happen," they say, "surely you are just crying 'Wolf'." Well, Jesus is the one who testified in Bible prophecy that there would in the last days come a great conspiracy by the devil and his human subjects (see Matthew 24). God's Word also reveals that the destruction of the saints will be a prime objective of this worldwide conspiracy: "And his power shall be mighty, but not by his own power: and he shall destroy wonderfully, and shall prosper, and practice, and shall destroy the mighty and the holy people" (Daniel 8:24).

So if we believe God's Word to be true and have faith in His ability to carry out His will, this fact becomes undeniable and unarguable: there *will* be a man with an elite circle of accomplices who will ascend to global prominence and leadership. According to Revelation 13:7 he and his small band of schemers will exercise control and power over *all* people and *all* nations. Now if that does not constitute a "conspiracy," perhaps we need to tell the scholars who put together the *Webster's Dictionary* to devise a new definition of the word "all."

Yes, the astounding truth is that God prophesied the coming of a conspiracy. Why then should we be surprised that as much as ten years ago, the New Age's Marilyn Ferguson entitled her bestselling guide and "bible" of the New Age *The Aquarian Conspiracy?* Moreover, some three years ago, Jose Arguelles, organizer of the internationally observed Harmonic Convergence, triumphantly boasted, "We are almost at the completion stage of bringing together all the thousands of New Age groups, organizations, and churches."[1]

Hidden Power: The Art and Science of Concealment

Conspirators realize that what they arc doing violates the norms of established society. Therefore, they invariably create *front organizations* to cover up their dirty work. Sometimes a front organization will front for yet another organization, which will be the cover for yet a third organization and so on down the chain. Thus, the real conspirators hide themselves behind a multiple number of layers, so that their operations will go undetected and their plans can succeed unobstructed. Often their existence is unknown even to the front organizations which take the heat when wrongdoing is found out. The real masters, stealthily hidden deep beneath the scene, usually go free and unscathed.

Freemasonry, for example, is only one of the many fronts and covers for The Order. Operating worldwide through thousands of Masonic groups and lodges, its real leadership works behind closed doors. Manley P. Hall, a 33rd degree Mason, in his book *Lectures on Ancient*

Philosophy, discloses how the masters of Masonry are able to conceal their anonymity and hide their maneuverings:

> Freemasonry is a fraternity within a fraternity--an outer organization concealing an inner brotherhood of the elect.... It is necessary to establish the existence of these two separate yet independent orders, the one visible and the other invisible.

> The *visible society* is a splendid camaraderie of free and accepted men enjoined to devote themselves to ethical, educational, fraternal, patriotic, and humanitarian concerns. The *invisible society* is a secret and most august fraternity whose members are dedicated to the service of a mysterious arcanum acandrum (defined as a secret; a mystery).

> In each generation, only a few are accepted into the inner sanctuary of the Work.... The great initiate-philosophers of Freemasonry are masters of that secret doctrine which forms the invisible foundations of every great theological and rational institution.[2]

Michael Howard, a man who has studied secret societies and orders from a secularist view (in other words, he does not have a Christian worldview), has written a thoroughly documented reference book entitled *The Occult Conspiracy: Secret Societies--Their Influence and Power In World History*. In this masterful work, Howard shows that the secret societies have deeply penetrated international politics. As the author shares, it is through the extraordinary efforts of the secret societies that "The history of the 20th century has been molded by a hidden power group."[3]

It is interesting that Howard actually favors the workings of these occult societies and endorses their efforts in building a one world government. According to him, "the hidden hands" of the conspiracy are rarely revealed to general view and when they are, it is "in a shadowy and indistinct form."[4]

A Conspiracy of Monumental Proportions

That a conspiracy exists and has served to shape world history is a foreign notion to many of us. It certainly was to me before I researched the truth of this matter. Yet, many years ago British Prime Minister Benjamin Disraeli noted that "The world is governed by very different personages from what is imagined by those who are not behind the scenes."

Moreover, as A. K. Chesterson writes in *The New Unhappy Lords,* "The proper study of political mankind is the study of power elites, without which nothing that happens could be understood."[5]

According to Chesterson, "These elites, preferring to work in private, are rarely found posed for photographers, and their influence upon events has therefore to be deduced from what is known of the agencies they employ." He continues, "Their goal was to work through such agencies, and financial support received from one or other or all three big American foundations--Rockefeller, Carnegie, and Ford--provides an infallible means of recognizing them."[6]

Adding a poignant footnote, Chesterson says that the conspirators invariably find no joy in their work, only a dull sensation and a numbing satisfaction on occasion: "Their doors are shut in the evenings; and they know no songs."

The Mainspring of Every Subversive Movement

Evidently, Winston Churchill, the great Prime Minister of Great Britain who led the English people through the dark days of World War II to victory over the Nazis, recognized the influence of this hidden conspiracy over world events. In the February 8, 1920 *Illustrated Sunday Herald* of London, he wrote:

> From the days of (Illuminati leader) Weishaupt to those of Karl Marx, to those of Trotsky, Bela Kuhn, Rosa Luxembourg, and Emma Goldman, this worldwide conspiracy has been steadily growing. This conspiracy has played a definitely recognizable role in the tragedy of the French Revolution. It has been the mainspring of every subversive movement during the 19th century; and now at last, this band of extraordinary personalities from the underworld of the great cities of Europe and America have gripped the Russian people by the hair of their heads, and have become practically the undisputed masters of that enormous empire.

Churchill also was able to discover through the intelligence services that Adolf Hitler had come to power through the aid of conspiratorial forces. He was no doubt fully aware that Hitler and his henchmen were members of the occultic Thule Society, a secret order which flourished in post-World War I Germany and was aided in its work with money provided by business and industrial interests.

But with the fall of Hitler, the rise of a prosperous Japan and Europe, and the current chaotic economic situation within the Soviet Union, is the same conspiracy alive and well today? Listen to the words of U.S. Senator Jesse Helms, Republican from North Carolina and the Senator probably most respected by conservative Christians today. Helms startled his colleagues in a speech two years ago on the floor of the United States Senate when he unmasked the invisible hand of the conspiracy by announcing, "These interests are working in concert with the masters of the Kremlin in order to create a New World Order."[7]

Secrets of The Illuminati

It was on May 1, 1776 that an Austrian named Adam Weishaupt founded the Order of the Illuminati in Bavaria. This was a highly secretive Masonic group that infamously sought the overthrow of the European monarchies so that it could establish its own leaders in power and accomplish its ultimate goal of one world government. Weishaupt and his conspirator associates' plans were fouled by the governments of his day, yet a number of writers have maintained that the Illuminati continued its operations around the world and that the same Illuminati is behind many of the major events occurring today which point to a conspiracy for a world order.

Could the Illuminati be behind today's conspiracy? This is a question that possibly is irrelevant because, as I have stated, the group of men whom I refer to as The Order have set up thousands of front organizations to cover their illegal operations. Yet, it is fascinating that a number of occult, New Age, and globalist organizations, perhaps in moments of weakness, refer approvingly to the Illuminati and speak eloquently of its goals and work.

In her book From Bethlehem to Calvary, Alice Bailey, founder of the Lucis Trust, speaks of the occult Messiah who is to come. He is described as "an illumined light-bearer . . . who can light the way for others." Moreover, Bailey makes this fascinating assertion:

> The Illuminati have ever led the race forward; the knowers, mystics, and saints have ever revealed to us the height of racial and individual possibilities.[8]

I do not believe that our use of the term *Illuminati* is important. The names of the various organizations created by The Order are designed to cause confusion and conceal what goes on inside The Order. In fact, the thousands of societies, organizations, groups, and churches funded and operated by The Order are all involved in a massive and intricately intertwined network. Many of those who lead these organizations and groups have no idea of the true source of their funding or even how they and their organizations fit into the overall plan. They are given just enough information to insure that their small part is played out with as much perfection and precision as possible.

Jose Arguelles, head of the Harmonic Convergence, alluded to this when he told an interviewer, "The now loose-knit features of a new world infrastructure will be brought into precision performance, establishing them as a globally cohesive command structure."[9]

The Knights Templar and Other Secret Societies

Meanwhile, writer Gaetan Delaforge, an authority on secret societies who is favorable to their objectives, in his book *The Templar Tradition and The Age Of Aquarius* suggests that The Order is in reality the old, medieval Knights Templar organization revived in a new and better form. He suggests that its goal is to:

> ... assist our world successfully to pass the present critical phase of its evolution in order that the Consciousness of Unity of All That Is, implanted in the planet by the creator and revitalized by the sanctified Cosmic Christ, can be realized within the allocated cycle.[10]

Actually, all of this is just so much mystical mumbo-jumbo intended to confuse us and get us off track in our investigation of The Order. Meanwhile, the magazine *Gnosis*, now popular in many occultic and New Age circles, recently published a series of articles showing that there has literally been an explosion of new secret societies and orders in Europe and the United States. Many of these groups are reported to have links with reactionary political and terrorist activities. Some involve themselves with neo-fascist festivals devoted to such mystical writers as J.R.R. Tolkien; others use celtic (druid/ pagan) crosses as rallying symbols.[11]

The Networking of Light Centers

Again, I caution the reader to beware of claims that one or another of these secretive societies is *the* mover-and-shaker behind the conspiracy. This is a multi-headed, serpentine monster which hides its evil but smoothly functioning black-hearted body behind a twisting and writhing mass of heads and tongues. The Order very effectively operates and conceals its work through a process called *networking*. Indeed, one group has even published a large book which contains some 1,526 organizations devoted to New Age goals that they are accomplishing through networking. The very title of this book is *Networking*.

Another such reference book is *The New Age Directory*, which lists 3,700 such groups including the Lucis Trust, Planetary Citizens, Futures Network, Findhorn Foundation, Office on Global Education, Ethics Network, Network of Light, World Federalists Association, World Union, and on and on.

Among the secret societies and orders, the many groups all working in tandem are referred to as *Light Centers*. Here is how two authorities describe the usefulness of such Light Centers:

Light Centers have developed into a worldwide network
that purposely link up...to serve as...receiving,
anchoring, and sending stations. Many such groups exist.[12]

The Lucis Trust and World Goodwill have identified
the men who run the conspiracy as networking members
of a special core group called *The New Group of World
Servers*. They are said to operate through a network of
ashrams, that name being taken from India where spiritual
centers operated by Hindu gurus are called ashrams. "The
union of all the Ashrams under the spiritual plan is
complete and the interlocking relationships will be
increasingly present," writes Alice Bailey.[13]

According to World Goodwill, the New Group of
World Servers are "enlightened ones whose right and
privilege it is to watch over human evolution and to guide
the destinies of men."[14]

Many, but not all of the secret societies and groups
which act as fronts and covers for the real Order also
attempt to operate in secrecy. Thus, the leader of one
such group first declares, "Now it is time for the world to
know that if it is to be saved, humans must adopt the same
government." Then this same man writes, "I cannot reveal
everything to you, it is too extraordinary, too incredible!"
He adds, "Even so, I am leading you step-by-step, further
and further into the science of the initiates."

This particular man is affiliated with a group called
the Universal White Brotherhood and presents what is
called the teachings of Agartha, a body of doctrine quite
similar to what Hitler and his Nazis of death once
believed.[15]

A Rose By Any Other Name

There is an old saw that goes like this, "A rose by any
other name is still a rose." Though The Order may hide

behind its proliferation of fronts and ardently seek to conceal its operations, still it is quite easy for a trained observer trusting in divine guidance to discern its workings. The Order always leaves behind tell-tale traces of its work. I learned long ago as an officer in the U.S. Armed Forces that we were never to listen to what the opposition said, but we were to simply keep our eyes on *what it does*. When we look at what the conspirators are doing, then we realize what it is we contend with.

Randall Baer, a former top New Age leader who became a born again Christian, best expressed the nature of the conspiracy we must contend with in his revealing bestseller, *Inside The New Age Nightmare*. He wrote:

> This agenda is nothing less than the complete revolution-izing of the very foundations of not only America but the entire world. Such a plan calls for the total restructuring of planetary civilization into an enlightened One World Federation in which national boundaries and sovereignty are secondary, and 'planetary citizenship' in the 'global village' is the order of the day. This (conspiracy) offers a world in desperate need a grand solution to profound global problems. Apparent world peace and unprecedented opportunities...are to be unveiled. Herein lies the Antichrist's last temptation, offered to all the world.[16]

For those who might claim that Randall Baer and Texe Marrs are simply sensationalists and contend that we are over-dramatizing the dangers of the massive conspiracy that confronts America and Christianity today, I would simply suggest that such critics and skeptics judge for themselves by reading the entirety of the chapters that follow in this book. After doing so, as I said, only an utter fool would deny that a conspiracy of unparalleled propor-tions is at work today in the world.

Perhaps the skeptic might also consider what hap-pened to Randall Baer after he became a Christian and determined to expose the New Age Movement and the conspiracy. The very same week Randall's thoroughly documented and authoritative book, *Inside the New Age Nightmare,* was to be released last year, he was found dead. Authorities in the state of Colorado reported that his car had mysteriously veered off the edge of a rocky cliff some 300 feet into the valley below. According to the police report, no alcohol nor illegal drugs of any nature were involved. Authorities are mystified and have no clues to the tragedy.

Who killed Randall Baer? Was foul play involved? We cannot say for sure; however, it is a documented fact that Randall was scheduled to be a guest on a number of important radio and TV programs in connection with the release of his important exposé. Whether or not he was murdered by members of the conspiracy is for you and I to ponder. But I do know that these evil men are certainly capable of such heinous acts. One of their own, Adolf Hitler, saw to the torture, brutality, and massacre of millions in concentration camps less than half a century ago.

Secret Societies and Other Conspiracies

For there is nothing covered that shall not be revealed; neither hid, that shall not be known. Therefore, whatsoever ye have spoken in darkness shall be heard in the light; and that which ye have spoken in the ear in closets shall be proclaimed upon the housetops.

(Luke 12:2-3)

I cannot reveal everything to you; it is too extraordinary, too incredible.

Omraam Aizonhov
Universal White Brotherhood

What I will prove in this book is that there is a subversive group of evil men whom I call The Order. The proof of this group's existence is found in the record of their activities on our planet. Their footprints can unmistakably be traced in the decisions now being made in several key areas of world finance, politics, and religion.

I realize of course that many will refuse to believe that such a conspiracy exists. Frankly, until a few years ago, I was one of the skeptics. But in studying what is called the New Age Movement intensely and with great concentration for almost five years now, I began to realize that the New Age Movement was only the *visible* manifestation of something quite *invisible* that was going on behind closed doors.

In other words, the New Age Movement, with its literally tens of thousands of networking and interlinking cult groups, churches, organizations, and societies, is only the *outward form* of something *hidden from view*. That something I have now come to realize is a small clique of fabulously wealthy men whose influence reverberates throughout the world.

Many Names, Same Conspiracy

We can justifiably call these men the *invisible college*. In fact, that is exactly one of the names which they have been dubbed. But a growing number of authorities, whether they be Christian, secular, or New Age, agree that there *is* such a conspiratorial group in existence. One New Age writer refers to them as the *Council of All Beings*. Marilyn Ferguson calls them members of the *Open Conspiracy*.[1] Elizabeth Claire Prophet, founder of the cultic Church Universal and Triumphant, proclaims them to be the *Great White Brotherhood*, while a man named Eklal Kueshana, leader of a mystical organization and community known as the Stelle Group, in his bestselling book *The Ultimate Frontier* identifies them simply as *The Brotherhood*.

Kueshana insists that their conspiracy is benign. In fact, he terms it "a grand, beneficent conspiracy of vital concern to an important segment of mankind."[2] He says that their primary goal is economic redistribution of all the world's resources, and he claims that *their work cannot be stopped*.

The ultimate victory of the conspirators, claims Kueshana, is assured. Moreover, he asserts that to achieve their aims, destruction and chaos will most certainly take place. He also suggests that Adolf Hitler was inspired by this group. According to what one member of the conspiracy told Kueshana, "Hitler is a product of a grand experiment which backfired."[3]

Benjamin Creme is the self-styled "John the Baptist" for a strange spirit from beyond whom Creme says is the World Teacher, Maitreya, the "Christ of the New Age." Creme says that the planet is ruled by 15 *Masters of Wisdom* who currently reside in the everyday world.[4]

Alice Bailey, who founded the Lucis Trust based on the teachings of the group known as Theosophy, gives yet another name to the concealed elite group who are said to secretly rule the world. "They are," she writes, "the *New Group of World Servers.*" The New Group of World Servers, according to Bailey, are working a certain Plan around the world through interlocking relationships. Their goal: "The custodians" of this Plan seek the establishment of a One World Government and a "New International Economic Order."[5]

John Randolph Price, head of the Planetary Commission and creative mind and organizer of the annual event called World Healing Day, also known as the Instant of Cooperation, World Meditation Day and Global Mind-Link, speaks of a *Council of Masters*. He says that this Council is "composed of certain superbeings who have risen above humanhood to become deities in their own right."[6] New Age authorities such as Price, Bailey, and Creme report that the group now in charge of overseeing the world's progress is itself being led by beings from the spirit world known variously as The Hierarchy, or as the Ascended Masters.

Another popular New Age proponent of a hidden group of "wise men" who control the world behind the scenes is Vera Stanley Alder of Great Britain. In her meticulously detailed books, *The Initiation of the World* and *When Humanity Comes Of Age*, Alder refers to these men as the *World Mind*. "They are," she reports, "the torch bearers of a New Age for men." Their objective is said to be the building of a new civilization from the ashes of the old:

> In the coming years, as the men who comprise the World Mind intently follow the guiding of their spirit masters from the mystical city or realm called Shamballa, the world will be reconstructed along entirely new lines.[7]

According to Djwhal Khul, one of the ascended masters channeled by Alice Bailey, the conspiracy is headed up by the *Custodians of The Plan.* Bailey maintains that the human custodians of The Plan are "occultly guarded." "Think not that I can tell you of the Plan as it truly is," Khul is said to have told Bailey, "it is a 'hidden secret.'"[8]

In his excellent book, *Guardians of the Grail,* Christian prophecy teacher J. R. Church authoritatively documents a conspiratorial group headquartered in Europe known by the same title as his book, *Guardians of the Grail.*[9] According to J. R., the Guardians of the Grail are successors to the Knight Templars, a military organization of warrior monks active in the Christian crusade against the Moslem occupation of the Holy Land.

The Templars were suppressed in 1312 on charges of heresy and magical practices and their leader burned at the stake. However, in one form or another, notably as the Priory of Sion, the Templars carried on their heinous activities. Today, in the form of the organization identified as the Guardians of the Grail, their number possibly includes Otto Von Hapsburg, of the Hapsburg dynasty and now an influential member of the European Parliament.

The Guardians of the Grail are wicked men who believe that Jesus and Mary Magdalene together conceived a child. They fancy themselves to be of this same holy bloodline. They also are followers of an occult doctrine which includes worship of the black goddess.

The Hidden Kings of Europe

I have carefully studied Otto Von Hapsburg and his colleagues. Von Hapsburg has long been a supporter of the Pan-European movement. He is an advocate of a new European order in which the nobility will be preeminent in places of leadership. The elderly Von Hapsburg is gaining in years now, but he has a son, Karl, who is most able to take up the slack. It is suggested that the young, handsome, and photogenic Karl Von Hapsburg could one day become the Antichrist, although clearly this is conjecture at this point.

We may hear more from these men and women of royal blood in the days ahead. One thing is for sure, Otto Von Hapsburg and other members of European royalty, whether deposed or still on the throne, constitute a surprisingly significant voice in today's Europe. These personages include King Michael, deposed monarch of Romania; Prince Carl Von Schwarzenberg, head of the noble house that once controlled Czechoslovakia, Prince Bernhard and Queen Juliana, who continue to reign in the Netherlands, Bulgaria's deposed King Simeon II, Greece's ousted King Constantine II, and several others. It is an axiom of history that history repeats itself.

Incidentally, Otto Von Hapsburg, who would now be King of Hungary had the Hapsburg empire not fallen, has been called "Europe's hidden king." He has also been quoted as saying: "The time for the dynasty lies in some happier tomorrow when a new Europe, purged by war, will undergo a time of resurrection."[10]

Otto Von Hapsburg has been extremely active in speaking to such groups as the Knights of Columbus, the Catholic equivalent to the Freemasons, and to other political and economic groups in Europe. Revealingly, he has a daughter named Walpurga, born in 1958. Is it a mere coincidence that *Walpurgisnacht* is one of the most holy days in the witch and Satanic calendar?

Are These Groups Front Organizations?

The Order is quite disingenuous and masterfully malevolent in the way in which it conceals its operations. As I have mentioned, it has created a number of front organizations. Through these fronts, The Order is able to divert the attention of those who seek to track its operations and who are working to expose and unmask its evil Plan. A quick look at some key organizations which I believe are fronts for The Order will give you an idea of how extensive is this cover-up and how adept is The Order in establishing front organizations to disguise its true purposes.

There is, for example, the *World Future Society*, which publishes the magazine *The Futurist* and has an interesting logo of what appears to be three sixes within a circle (or 666). Another group which receives a lot of publicity today is known as *The Planetary Initiative For The World We Choose*. This group, as do most front organizations of The Order, operates out in the open. Its members include Norman Cousins, who is also head of yet another front group, World Federalists; Robert F. Drinan, Catholic priest and formerly a U.S. Congressman; Donald Fraser, mayor of Minneapolis; Reverend Theodore Hesburgh, chancellor of Notre Dame University; Isaac Asimov, the noted science fiction author; and the Dalai Lama, the Buddhist spiritual guru of Tibet.

The Planetary Initiative For The World We Choose is the organization which came up with the catchy slogan now echoed by almost every globalist environmental group active today: "Think globally, act locally." In their ignorance (hopefully!) a number of Christian organizations, and even Dr. Leighton Ford, the top lieutenant to Billy Graham, have pushed this same slogan as a real neat idea for the church to demonstrate its concern for world environmentalism.

Another possible project of The Order is the *Better*

World Society, whose chief honcho is Ted Turner of Cable News Network (CNN). The Better World Society has a number of distinguished members, one of whom is Jimmy Carter, former president of the United States of America.

The Council on Foreign Relations: Kingpin of the Conspiracy?

An organization that many researchers of the conspiracy believe to be the primary mover for The Order is the *Council on Foreign Relations (CFR).* Among its influential, moneyed leadership: Walter Wriston, formerly chairman, Citicorp/Citibank, America's largest banking institution; Howard Baker, former chief of staff to the president of the United States of America and Senator from the state of Tennessee; Abba Eban, former Israeli ambassador to the United Nations and that country's foreign minister; George Schultz, Secretary of State under President Ronald Reagan; Cyrus R. Vance, former Secretary of State under President Jimmy Carter; E. Nukazawa, head of the Federation of Economic Organizations for Japan; and Lieutenant-General Brent Scowcroft, a diplomat, U.S. arms negotiator, and former military officer who was vice-chairman of what is probably *the* premier CFR group, Kissinger Associates, headed by Henry Kissinger, former Secretary of State under President Nixon and himself a member of CFR. Oh yes, there is also David Rockefeller, Sr., who is suspected by many of being the chief cog in the conspiratorial network.

The Council on Foreign Relations publishes a journal, *Foreign Affairs,* and conducts seminars which are attended by elitist financiers, bankers, industrialists, media managers, and politicians from around the globe. It's goal has long been the creation of a One World Order.

The Trilateral Commission and its Role in the Conspiracy

Another group infamous for its goal of uniting Japan, Europe, and the United States into one grand entity to promote a world order is the *Trilateral Commission (TLC)*. Many see the membership and work of the Trilateral Commission as the nucleus of The Order. But again, what we have here is a "tail of the dog" situation. TLC is simply one of a number of connected, interwoven, and interlocking groups founded by The Order. Significantly, many top officials of the TLC also serve in key positions of influence in other related organizations.

Former U.S. Senator and presidential candidate Barry Goldwater, in his book *With No Apologies,* explains that "whereas the Council on Foreign Relations is distinctly national in membership, the Trilateral Commission is international. Representation is allocated equally among Western Europe, Japan, and the United States (and Canada)."[11]

Senator Goldwater adds this chilling note about the Trilateral Commission: "It is intended to be the vehicle for multinational consolidation of the commercial and banking interests by seizing control of the political government of the United States."[12] How much more plain can a senator in-the-know be?

Moreover, Goldwater contends that "Zbigniew Brzezinski, former chairman of the National Security Agency and National Security Council under President Carter, and megabanker and multimillionaire David Rockefeller *screen and select every individual* who is invited to participate in shaping and administering the proposed New World Order."[13]

Senator Goldwater concludes that:

> The Trilateral Commission represents a skillful, coordinated effort to seize control of and consolidate the four

centers of power--political, monetary, intellectual, and ecclesiastical.... What the trilateralists truly intend is the creation of a world-wide economic power superior to the political governments of the nation-states involved ... As managers and creators of the system they will control the future.[14]

Reliable sources indicate that Mikhail Gorbachev recently met with the prominent members of the Trilateral Commission at the Kremlin in Moscow. Subsequently, he gave a speech at the United Nations which showed clearly that his proposals were virtually identical to those of globalists, including the TLC, working toward a New World Order.[15]

The Knights of Malta: Arm of the Vatican?

Another quite different group that my research indicates is deeply involved in the activities and plans of The Order is a strange yet significant organization known as the Sovereign Military Order of Malta, or SMOM. This group is intimately linked with international Freemasonry and with the men whom J.R. Church calls the "Guardians of the Grail." Its membership call themselves *Knights of Malta*. One of these knights, the late William Casey, was appointed by President Ronald Reagan as director of the Central Intelligence Agency. Another, James Buckley, was chief of U.S. propaganda against Eastern Europe as leader of Radio Free Europe/Radio Liberty. J. Peter Grace, the wealthy industrialist who was once accused of bringing Nazi war criminals to America, heads up North American operations for the Knights of Malta.[16]

Reportedly, membership of the Knights of Malta numbers more than 70,000. Significantly, its main office is at the Vatican, and Pope John Paul II is a top supporter who has praised the work of the Knights in a special proclamation.[17]

President Bush and the Skull and Bones Society

Some of the richest men in the world are Knights of Malta. Among them, former U.S. Secretary of the Treasury William Simon, fast becoming a billionaire due to his acquisition of failed savings and loans, which he supposedly rehabilitates, and President George Bush's brother, Prescott Bush, Jr.

It should be noted that President George Bush, now a member of the Council on Foreign Relations, was a Trilateralist (TLC), and while at Yale was initiated into a strange, arcane, possibly pro-Nazi secret society known as *Skull and Bones*.[18] Skull and Bones chooses only 15 graduates of Yale each year to be initiated into its secret organization. However, these men continue to promote the Brotherhood and guide each other's destiny throughout the remainder of their lives.

A woman invader into the Skull and Bones sanctuary saw "a literal Nazi shrine." She also stated that "one room on the second floor has a bunch of swastikas, kind of an SS macho iconography." "Somebody," she exclaimed, "should ask George Bush about the swastikas in there."[19] Her story was confirmed by three other Yale University women who infiltrated the Skull and Bones sanctuary and went through its artifacts and occult paraphernalia.

The logo of Skull and Bones is that of a skull and bones with the cryptic and mysterious number "322" underneath. No one knows for sure exactly what the 322 means or stands for. Carefully documented research by Anthony Sutton, outlined in his authoritative book, *The Skull And Bones Society*, has demonstrated that this group was no doubt originally the brainchild of an esoteric, deeply hidden secretive society based in Germany.

According to another source, the number 322 derives from 322 B.C., the date of the death of the great Greek orator Demosthenes, who founded a society from which Skull and Bones is said to have its origin. It should be noted that in the name of Demosthenes is the root, *demos*, of the word *democracy*. However, check your dictionary and you will find that this greek root word, demos, means *mob rule.*[20]

At least one other book has been written on this bizarre cultic society, the Skull and Bones, into which President George Bush, Winston Lord, former ambassador to China, and U.S. Senators David Boren of Oklahoma and John Chaffe of Rhode Island, among others, have been initiated. That book, by researchers Walter Isacsson and Evan Thomas, is titled *The Wise Men.*

Intrigue At The Vatican

That the Vatican and the Pope might be involved in the dark labyrinth of the secret societies may shock some readers. But those who have studied carefully the history of the Vatican and its dealings with secret societies over the centuries are not at all surprised. For many years the Vatican has maintained links with the various brotherhoods, orders, and secret societies that have flourished throughout Europe and the Middle East.

Some of the Catholic orders--for instance, the Jesuits-- have themselves carried out secret operations and missions. A number of popes promoted the Great Crusades and during that era, the Knights Templar literally became a functionary of the Vatican--its designated agent in a holy war against the Moslems. In addition, mountainous evidence can be marshalled to demonstrate that today the Vatican is heavily infiltrated and influenced by Masonic interests.[21]

Though space is too limited here to go into greater detail, I intend in a subsequent book to more exhaustively reveal the ongoing intrigue at the Vatican and its startling connections with agents of The Order.

Conspiracies Are Natural Occurrences

While the general public believes that conspiracies are rare and their circumstances mysterious, actually, a conspiracy is in the natural order of things. Lucifer began it all when he cunningly conspired against God. Failing in his scheme, he nevertheless was able to persuade one-third of the angels in Heaven to go along with his evil plot. Then, cast down to earth, he brought in Eve as an accomplice. Admittedly, she was an unwitting accomplice. Still, Eve disobeyed God and conspired with the devil for her own purposes. Then she went out and got *another* new convert, Adam, and they *colluded together.* Men and women, it seems, are *natural* lawbreakers ... and *natural* conspirators as well.

The Mastermind Behind Conspiracies

Satan is a mastermind and inspirer of conspiracies. The Bible makes this crystal clear. It was by *conspiracy* that Jesus was killed. The Jewish leaders and the Sanhedrin plotted His death. They were even able to plant a spy in His midst--Judas, one of the twelve men in the world closest to our Lord. This was also a *money-driven* conspiracy: Judas was given 30 pieces of silver for his contribution to the conspiracy.

The schemers next brought a reluctant Pilate into their conspiracy. His motive was power, an intangible resource that he feared he might lose if a rebellion were to break out by associates of Jesus, who was accused by the Jews of plotting to become King and overthrow the Romans who then occupied Israel.

In the book of Acts, at Ephesus, we read of another *money conspiracy*. There, silversmiths and merchants plotted the death of Paul because they were afraid that their goddess Diana would lose popularity and they would lose money by not being able to sell crafts and souvenirs based on her worship. Indeed, all of the apostles were the target of conspirators among the pharisees, Judaizers, and the followers of Nero and those who succeeded him as Caesars of Rome.

Political Conspiracies Can Prove Deadly

Through *conspiracy*, Hitler was able with just a few evil men to seize control of the apparatus of an entire modern nation. A member of the secretive Thule Society, Hitler went on to initiate and oversee a World War that inflicted tens of millions of casualties and caused untold suffering and horror.

The same was true of Lenin in Russia. The Marxist conspiracy of Lenin was of international scope. It is known that Lenin received financial aid and encouragement from certain European monarchs who encouraged him to do his dirty work in Russia. Significantly, Lenin realized that the majority of the Russian people would not willingly back his radical brand of socialism. Therefore, he established what he called the "Dictatorship of the Proletariat" as a seed group to push forward his plans for dictatorial control of the vast Russian empire.

This, then, was a *conspiracy* led by a small but determined group willing to use money--or murder--to gain its objectives. And what were its objectives? In a word, control of *money* and the use of it. Lenin claimed his was a war and revolution against men of money, the capitalists. In effect, an entire society in Russia, as well as the hundreds of millions of people in China and elsewhere who eventually became slaves of similar Marxist conspiracies, were victimized because of men's lust for money.

George Washington and other Conspirators

The American revolutionary heroes were conspirators against King George of England. In fact, they defiantly admitted their lawlessness, knowing full well that their *conspiracy* would cost them their lives if it failed. Indeed, if the British had won, each of the American "scoundrels and traitors," as they were then called by the King and the loyalists, would have made quick trips to the gallows. Because these men proved successful, history approvingly rewards them such epithets as "hero" and "fathers of their country."

Interestingly, the origins of this rebellion can also be traced, at least partially, to money ("taxation without representation.")

And More Conspiracies ...

Today we are literally inundated with *conspiracies*. The mafia and other criminals operate drug rings and money laundering operations, colluding with corrupt bankers, reprobate air pilots, and tin-horn dictators in Central and South America for filthily earned greenbacks. They are conspirators.

Government regulators are constantly indicting stock market manipulators and insiders. Many are not caught, however, because they pay off the regulators and influence congressmen through illegal campaign contributions. Again, these are all evidences of *conspiracies* at work. And there is more such evidence.

The Watergate *conspirators* brought down the President of the United States and he was ousted from office in disgrace. Price fixing by automobile makers, oil companies, and airlines is epidemic and their collusion together behind closed doors is the mark of a *conspiracy*. J. Edgar Hoover, Director of the FBI, wrote his famous book, *Masters of Deceit*, in which he exposed the workings of the worldwide communist spy network: a *conspiracy*. Indeed, the Central Intelligence Agency, the British Secret Service, the Israeli Mossad, and other intelligence agencies are involved in *conspiracies*. Such agents conspire together, using fake I.D.'s, secret passwords, codes and ciphers, disguises, ruses, secretive handshakes and other signals, as well as electronic surveillance, spy satellites, and cryptographic equipment to achieve their conspiratorial purposes.

Not too long ago, the wealthy Hunt brothers of Dallas conspired together to corner the world's silver market. Their insider's *conspiracy* was not successful, however, and they ended up bankrupt.

Common Characteristics of Conspirators

It can be seen that there are at least five common characteristics of conspirators. *First*, if they are successful in their conspiring, they may well become much admired role models and heros, or even world leaders; many will also gain great affluence and join the ranks of the wealthy and decadent. A *second* characteristic is that the plans and schemes of the conspirators are usually formulated secretly behind closed doors. A conspiracy is a private covenant between partners. *Third*, conspirators often use wealth and power to influence government officials and even to bring entire governments into their conspiracy. *Fourth*, they spread out the money liberally to gain influence and access.

Fifth, although occasionally their motives are worthwhile, noble, and altruistic, most often the motives of conspirators are extremely selfish. Simply stated, they lust after power and hunger for riches. As the Bible so wisely reminds us, "For the love of money is the root of all evil..." (I Timothy 6:10).

The Order is a master at carefully orchestrating for its own tremendous advantage all five of these characteristics of conspiracies. And as we have seen, it accomplishes much of its work through front organizations. In the next chapter we will study the devious work of yet more such groups--those designed to influence and to sway public opinion and thus prepare the world for the final assault.

THREE

When the Light Hits, the Dark Gets Tough

And the merchants of the earth shall weep and mourn over her; for no man buyeth their merchandise any-more... For in one hour so great riches is come to naught.

(Revelation 18:11, 17)

The distinct possibility of a major economic collapse and depression marks the end of history as we know it.

Jose Arguelles
Magical Blend

The many organizations, groups, and secret societies that comprise The Order and its "network of light" are now mounting an intensive, unparalleled campaign of propaganda. This campaign is designed to convince us that the only solution to today's complicated and perilous world problems is that offered by The Order: the globalism alternative--a One World Order led by a strong, universally acknowledged "wise" leader.

This unrelenting campaign is also intended to soften up the world and condition the masses for the gigantic blows to the economy that lie just ahead. It is expected that the advance "inside" information and predictions of The Order's front men and organizations will, in retrospect, be viewed by thinking people as evidence of the wisdom and leadership possessed by such groups and their leaders.

Once the world sinks into financial chaos and fear and panic seize the public, it is expected that anxious, quite possibly desperate men and women will turn to these "experts" and ask *them* to take over institutions and quell the crisis by implementing their proposed unified New World Order.

This alone should clue us in to the insidious and deceptive nature of the evil men who plot the conspiracy that confronts us. These men are the very ones who have created the financial chaos and chilled the world's economies in the first place, and they are to be the ones the whole world turns to for solutions! It is exactly this kind of dialectical situation and paradox in which The Order specializes.

Let us now examine some of the more important and influential propaganda organs supportive of the grand design of The Order.

The Economic Blueprint of the Hierarchy

The books published by the Lucis Trust are particularly enlightening. Alice A. Bailey, founder of the Lucis Trust, actually revealed in the *Externalization of the Hierarchy* a brief outline of the economic plan of The Order. She also revealed its three major avenues of attack: "The three main channels through which the preparation of the New Age is going on might be regarded as the Church, the Masonic Fraternity, and the educational field."[1]

This coincides with my own findings that a great apostasy is now occurring within the Church and a movement is brewing to bring all the world's religions into

WHEN THE LIGHT HITS, THE DARK GETS TOUGH ☐ 53

one. At the same time our schools have been infiltrated with occultic doctrines. The greatest achievement, however, of the Hierarchy, that shadowy group of demonic entities which oversees the conspiracy, is in the area of what Bailey has called the "Masonic Fraternity." Here she is referring not only to the various orders of Freemasonry, but to all secret societies in general, for there is an on-going networking among the various orders, brotherhoods and fraternities that together are loosely identified as the "Masonic Fraternity."

Bailey goes on to say that certain "adepts" (initiates) who are "authorities of modern financial matters" have prepared to "inaugurate a system of barter and exchange." This system, she says, will "supercede big business and private enterprise."[2] There is also to be a "complete economic reorientation" by which "humanity is relieved of all economic anxiety."[3]

Moreover, Bailey maintains that there will be an "all-over financial adjustment: the principal of sharing will be a recognized motivating concept of the new civilization." Interestingly, Bailey adds that "when the *adjuster of finances* appears, national currencies will have been largely superceded... by a universal monetary exchange."

And just how will this mystery man who is to act as the *adjuster of finances* accomplish the implementation of this new universal system?

Bailey's answer is that :

... all of the assets of the nation-states, as well as the various commodities, and all the organs of private enterprise, as well as public utilities and indeed all of planetary wealth--iron, steel, oil and wheat, for instance--will be owned... by a governmental, consulting international group... under international direction.[4]

To implement this bold plan it will be necessary to *destructure civilization*. In other words, tear down and destroy the current financial institutions in order to bring up from out of their ashes the new One World system under the firm control of what Bailey calls the "controlling international group."

Earth Day Workers Preach of Economic Collapse

Jose Arguelles was a leader in the recent Earth Day, 1990 celebration and was the mastermind of the worldwide Harmonic Convergence of 1987. Arguelles has said that the latter event kicked off a five-year plan which includes the *purification* of the earth and the work of *destructuring civilization*. To accomplish this, Arguelles and others are working to gain the support of intellectuals through the process of *networking*.

The success of this endeavor is apparent. As Jose Arguelles told one New Age magazine, "We are almost at the completion stage of bringing together all of the thousands of New Age groups, organizations, and churches."[5]

Evidently Jose Arguelles and other front men for the secret societies are actively preaching that an *economic collapse* is coming. They are preparing their disciples for a stock market crash, the issuing of the new money, and the organizing of the New International Economic Order. These people have evidently been told of at least some of the economic events that are soon to occur so that they can prepare their people for the rapid-fire succession of events and better gain an advantage.

Jose Arguelles, for example, told one interviewer, "The next few years are going to be *rough weather*. It is important that people be aware of this and prepare their lifeboats, as the industrial civilizations are passengers on a sinking ship." Arguelles also warned his followers that "the distinct possibility of a major economic collapse and depression marks the end of history as we know it."[6]

Revealingly, Jose Arguelles advises his listeners to

always remember this maxim: "When the light hits, the dark gets tough."[7] Members of The Order and their lower echelon organizations claim to be "the light." So Arguelles is apparently warning his cohorts to expect opposition to the coming financial, political, and social changes from those whom he characterizes as "the dark."

Lord Maitreya Predicts Stockmarket Crash

Even Benjamin Creme and his internationalist Tara Center seem to be getting a glimmer of what is soon to transpire, although I believe that neither he nor his so-called "Christ", the Lord Maitreya, are in the inner circle of the international elite. Creme is simply a mouth and a showman, yet he seems to be aware of some key events on The Order's secret agenda. In his group's publication *Share International News* recently was the stunning headline, "Stock Market Crash." "A world stock market crash," read the article, "will begin in Japan. Maitreya says that the stock market crash is inevitable. The end is in sight."[8]

According to Creme's Maitreya, "The impending stock market crash is an outcome of commercialization." In Maitreya's view, said the magazine, commercialization means "making money while others starve."

Another article in *Share International* remarked that after the coming stock market crash, "The stock markets as they are now run will have no place in the new society."[9] This comment is, of course, understandable since it has long been the goal of Creme and his friends to establish a Socialist World Society.

Creme has also announced that "Within some weeks or at most months after the stock market crash, Maitreya expects to give a world press conference which in turn leads to the Day of Declaration, then he will leave no doubt that he is the World Teacher."

And More Propaganda Initiatives

Other front people and organizations also are spear-heading the propaganda initiative. For example, the World Future Society, which includes on its board of directors Orville Freeman, former U.S. Secretary of Agriculture; Barbara Marx Hubbard, noted New Age author; Robert McNamara, former president of the World Bank; and Irving Shapiro, former chairman of DuPont, the corporate chemical giant. In a letter to its thousands of members the World Future Society forecasted six key events to occur over the next 25 years. Forecast number five was as follows: "A worldwide economic collapse is extremely likely in the next few years. Those unprepared may stand naked before a crisis unseen in the U.S. since the Civil War."

This unusual prediction of the World Future Society is echoed by the dire warnings of Richard Lamm, former governor of Colorado, in a commentary he wrote for *The Republic*. Lamm, a darling of New Agers and a favored speaker at singer John Denver's Windstar Community, is the man who once suggested that the "elderly should go ahead and die because it is costing too much to take care of them." His commentary in *The Republic* was headlined, "U.S. Will Pay for Its Excesses."[10]

Lamm is one of those who sees America as the big, bad bully in all things and he seems to take pride in slamming America. "America faces a self-imposed day of reckoning," Lamm wrote. "We have planted the seeds of decline and we shall harvest the results . . . we have made too many mistakes. Our excesses are too deep. The Piper shall have to be paid."

Lamm forecasts a number of traumas for America and contends that "the first trauma is an *economic* one." He predicts a crash in real estate prices, including residential homes, and the bankruptcy of banks, savings and loans, and insurance companies on a widespread scale. He also says the federal deficit will soar and that the dollar will have to be severely devalued.

Naturally, Lamm has the answer to our difficulty. We simply need to adjust to the need to come into unity with the "New World marketplace," an acronym of the internationalists who really desire that America become slaves of foreign powers and that our nation dissolve its national borders and be merged with the new One World Order.

What Do They Know That We Don't?

What do people like Alice Bailey, Benjamin Creme, Richard Lamm, the influential directors of the World Future Society and similar spokespersons and groups know that most Americans do not? This is a key question that we should ponder, for over the last decade Americans have been told that a bright new future is on the horizon, that the economic bad times are a thing of the long forgotten past. When George Bush and Mikhail Gorbachev met in their superpower summit meetings, the press releases from the White House and the Kremlin suggested that a brave new world order was at hand and that an unprecedented era of peace and prosperity was practically guaranteed. The awful truth was far different. As I meticulously document in this book, the financial understructure of America is rotten and the financial safety net is virtually eaten up.

Meanwhile, in the Soviet Union things are even worse. That nation's economic system--if one could call it a *system*--is so rickety that its citizens are falling through the cracks. The whole thing is ready to go up in an explosion at any time because of the building anger of the people who have been deprived for so long of the fruits of their labors.

The answer to the question, what do people like

Bailey, Creme, and others know that we don't, is simply this: they realize that *there is a network of high-level, wealthy industrialists and bankers whose chief goal is the creation of a superstate which their own handpicked leader will rule with an iron hand.* Benjamin Creme would be the first to admit the existence of this secretive group; he has remarked:

> There is a group of high initiates--industrialists, economists and administrators of great experience and achievements-- who, with the Hierarchy, have worked out plans and blue- prints that will solve the redistribution problems of the world, when the *political will* is there to implement them.[11]

According to Creme, all that is needed for the wealthy schemers to achieve their long cherished goals is *political will.* The men at the top of the secret societies realize that they must marshal the will of the masses for their One World project to succeed. In today's world it is extremely difficult to establish totalitarian control without at least some cooperation from the people who are to be ruled. The greatest dictators of human history were keenly aware of this fact and so they worked to create a form of mass hysteria among the people, rousing their emotions, their lustful desires, their imperialistic ambitions, and their greed for money and materialism.

Hitler promised the German people a Third Reich which would last for at least 1,000 years. Stalin launched his monstrous collectivization campaign with the promise of a New Soviet Man, and unparalleled prosperity far beyond what the capitalist nations could achieve. Ruth- less tyrants such as Atilla the Hun, Genghis Kahn and the Caesars offered the people booty and riches, conquest, and power. What will the czars of the New World Order offer the people?

When Hitler came to power the German nation was in the throes of a terrible economic depression. He first offered them relief from their misery, and then with each victory of his stormtroopers through military conquest, he offered the masses the riches of pride and territorial imperialism. The point is that determined, ruthless tyrants are able to turn chaos into advantage for power. Their best opportunity comes during *economic crisis* when the frustrated and frightened are looking for a savior with a solution.

The Order Will Have The Answers

Now let's see what will be offered America and the world over the next few years by The Order. It is necessary first that there be a great economic depression, a money crash, and an ensuing financial panic. At exactly that moment the men who run The Order, through their propaganda organs and fronts, will offer seemingly reasonable, even marvelous solutions to the crisis. They will say, "America will have to pay for its excesses, but we have the answers; give us power and let us put into place our new systems, and the financial problems will all be resolved and a general prosperity assured."

Alice Bailey alluded to this in her Lucis Trust book, *Esoteric Psychology*, in which she fully acknowledged that the "builders of the new civilization" must "make their presence felt *immediately after a crisis has occurred.*"[12] She says that certain "Masters are working strenuously in the world of business and of finance." Further, she explains that their methods cannot be revealed in her book: "It is not possible to enlarge within a brief space upon the methods and the plans of the Hierarchy at this time of crisis and emergency in connection with the field of money."

However, she does enlighten us to the *method* these Masters of business and finance will use to gain the popular authority needed to build the new civilization.

"The general method employed," she writes, *"is one of inspiration and of the presentation of moments of crisis."[13]*

Significantly, she adds: "These moments offer opportunity for the activity of some disciple."

Who this *disciple* is Bailey does not say. In any case, he is to be the one who leads the members of the secretive group that the Lucis Trust has termed the "New Group of World Servers." I am convinced that this mysterious and esoteric New Group of World Servers is simply another synonym and code-phrase for the hidden members of The Order.[14]

The Dollar Will Have To Go!

According to The Order, after the crash the first thing necessary to return prosperity to all will be *a new currency.* The dollar has to go. This is, for instance, the view held by the Aspen Institute which has solid ties to the CFR, TLC, and the United Nations through its membership. This group's financial supporters include the Rockefellers, the Carnegie Corporation, the Ford Foundation, and others. Its trustees include Robert McNamara and Henry Kissinger. In an interview, Joseph Slater, then president of Aspen Institute, proposed "that there be a council of wise persons that can figure out how to restructure national government and achieve economic and social values."[15]

We can best understand exactly what Slater and the Aspen planners have in mind when we further read his announcement that, "We cannot go on with the dollar." We note also his suggestion that the world be managed by a "consortium of the concerned."[16]

That the Aspen Institute has tremendous power in these areas of finance is unchallenged. In 1990, for example, President George Bush and Britain's Prime

Minister Margaret Thatcher met under the auspices of the Aspen Institute to discuss various economic and political issues. Many other world leaders have also trekked to Aspen, Colorado, to participate in various seminars, forums, and conferences sponsored by the group.

Only A One World Order Can Suffice

The Club of Rome (COR), which has also been fingered as one of the top conspiratorial groups, is another pusher of a One World Economic Order. The COR has stated that "only a global revolution, the substitution of a New World Economic Order, can save us."[17] To assure such a world order, the past leader of the COR, the late Aurelio Peccei, proposed that a "charismatic leader... would be the world's only salvation from the social and economic upheaval that threatens to destroy civilization."[18]

Was this some off-the-wall comment by an insignificant propagandist? When we consider that the COR's founding leader, Peccei, was a member of the Bilderbergers and that the Rockefellers, New Age bestselling author John Naisbitt *(Megatrends)*, World Federalist head Norman Cousins, former Bank of America Chairman Louis Rundhorn, and similar globalists are involved in its programs, we begin to see the picture.

Now We Enter the Era of Warriors

The dread economic specter that lies ahead is perhaps best expressed by Dr. Ravi Batra, an economist who wrote the number one *New York Times* bestseller, *The Great Depression of 1990.* Batra, who has called for a Socialist

World State, writes in his book that we are now entering the "era of warriors."[19] Our political and social structures must change to accommodate this new era, he says. "In the Warrior Age, the Army, headed by a dictator--king, emperor, president--controls the government as well as society. Political authorities centralize in the form of an absolute government, people are highly disciplined... and so on."[20]

Batra also asserts that we are about to go into a period of terrible economic chaos which will result in a complete overhauling of our political and social structure.

Revealingly enough, Batra's ideas have been endorsed by writers from *Fortune* magazine, *The New York Times, The Dallas Morning News* and other media propaganda tools. It is also interesting that Batra first published his book under his own imprint, Venus Books, showing clearly that he is a believer in the Goddess. What's more, Batra, a Hindu, admits that his economic "wisdom" comes from spirit entities whom he contacts during meditation.

It is sad but significant that the minds of the public have been so conditioned that they will almost break down the turnstiles rushing into bookstores to read the economic advice and warnings of a man who admittedly bases his writings on Hinduism and is a medium to the spirit world.

Is The Era of Solar Man Dawning?

Batra is joined in his austere warning by Thomas Ehrenzeller, a director of the World Federalist Association, in his book *Solar Man*. Here are just a few "nuggets" from Ehrenzeller's book which, in fact, is simply a PR guide to the conspirators' plan for a New World Order:

> As the sun rises on the coming age, we see a great task before us. What we see is the final, most critical stage in

the maturation and civilization of man. A great human civilization is to be built ... The U.S. has major responsibilities, both regionally and globally, to the just world system which is to come.

There is a New Europe coming ... Russia may be a part of that New Europe. ... Today a reinvigorated West Germany has become an integral part of a European Community that is the economic equal of either superpower, and may soon be their equal politically, as well. At the other end, the Soviets face a Japan of similarly renewed vigor.

The holocaust that hangs over our heads is the price we pay if we do not learn to live together. No demon or monster placed that threat over our heads. We did it ourselves ... we must deal with the demons of our own creation or they will destroy us.

World unity alone can create permanent world peace. ... Tired of war, the people of the world will rise up and demand their rights to universal peace and freedom ...

The era in which the people of the world finally cast off the bonds of nationalistic self-deception, freeing themselves to join together in one free community, will be a true Solar Age. As solar citizens we will be part of one mighty race. ... We can build a mighty Solar Nation, a nation of nations. ... The people will lose nothing. They will only gain.

World government will have the power to do that which only world government can do: secure every nation from aggression and eliminate the threatening cloud of nuclear annihilation that hangs over all our heads.

We could build a World Society ... and so we will. ... There is no force that can stop such a movement if the broad masses of people around the world can be aroused to strive positively for the cause of world democracy. Human society must finally become one single society, united in its diversity.... The New Era is coming, whether the guardians of the old are ready or not.[21]

Whether We Want It Or Not

The outline of what is planned for us by The Order thus becomes clear. First, for over a decade the leaders of the various secret societies and organizations, most funded and controlled by The Order, have been conditioning us that a great economic catastrophe is soon to occur. This catastrophe will also involve at least a major limited war of some kind with great casualties and suffering by some of the world's peoples. This will convince people everywhere that a radical solution is needed to solve the immediate crisis.

Solutions already proposed by The Order include a One World Currency, open borders leading to no borders, the sharing and redistribution of all the world's resources (take from the rich nations and give to the poor), the submergence and impoverishment of the United States and North America, and the ascendancy and supremacy of Europe and, at a lesser level, Japan.

To shock the nations into action, the agenda of The Order calls for a war which will usher in the new, more desirable "warrior era." This war is needed to cleanse and purify earth and prepare it for the coming radiant New Age. In essence, The Order is going to create a horrendous crisis which will give them, the elite, the opportunity it needs to bring in its Plan. This Plan will be propagandized to the world as necessary for an unparalleled era of peace and prosperity. Of course, it will also be seen as necessary that those who have brought the world to this chasm must be dealt with decisively.

The Scapegoats Are Identified

And *who* might it be that has supposedly brought the world to the threshold of disaster? *Who* is it that The Order will paint as the scapegoats who caused the crisis? Naturally, it will be those who have in the past continued to call for patriotism and true democracy instead of the counterfeit One World Democratic Order, and the fundamentalist Christians who refuse unity, insisting instead on the exclusive nature of Jesus Christ as Lord of all. These will be the ones who opposed unity, and they will be fingered as threats to world peace, security, and prosperity.

Already the masses are being conditioned to take the steps necessary for the cleansing and purification actions that will be required by the money masters who will lead the world into the bright and radiant New Order. We of the "Old Order" will have to be purged.

In my book *Mystery Mark of the New Age*, I expose the malignant scheme of the New Age hierarchs to do away with those of us who resist their idea of unity. For example, I quoted Christopher Hyatt, head of the Order of the Golden Dawn, who suggested ways to deal with "the Christian fundamentalist problem." Hyatt told an interviewer that there would be a changing of the guards, and that bloodshed would have to be required:

> The guards of the ancient era ... the one dying right now ... are not willing to give up their authority so easily. I perceive, on a mass scale, that the New Age is not going to come into being as so many people believe and wish to believe. I see it as requiring a heck of a lot of blood, disruption, chaos and pain for a mass change to occur.[22]

We find in the popular writings of Ruth Montgomery additional documentation of the plans to rid the world of the resisters. Montgomery's books have literally sold in the millions, which means that all of her readers are prepared mentally for the steps that must be taken to enforce the new system of unity. Called by some the Herald of the New Age, Montgomery claims that her spirit guides have given her this shocking revelation: There will be a shift of the earth caused by a great war that is to come. "Millions will survive and millions won't. Those who won't will go into the spirit state."[23]

Montgomery proclaims that once the millions of unfit are dealt with, then there will be an age which will "bring joy and happiness unexcelled since the days of the Atlantean era." But, she trumpets, only those whose minds are "open to the reality of one world will be around to enjoy it."[24]

Meanwhile, the millions of readers who have read the works of Alice Bailey are being programmed to believe that death isn't really a big thing anyway, and that the destruction and human carnage required to meet the crisis and establish a New Order is justifiable in light of the wonderful goals that are to be achieved. Bailey's master from beyond, Djwhal Khul, maintains "Death is not a disaster to be feared; the work of the Destroyer is not cruel or undesirable . . . therefore, there is much destruction permitted by the Custodians of the Plan and much evil turned into good."[25]

That it is Christian fundamentalists and Jews alike who are targeted is made clear by these ominous comments of Thomas Ehrenzeller, a director of the World Federalists:

Those who fall back to old-time religions are trying to hide in the past when things were simpler and less thought was required . . . Such timidity is unacceptable. We have to face the world as it is, doing what is necessary to save it.

A growing number of people . . . are sponsoring a backlash against the wave of religious fundamental fanaticism . . . The right course to take is that which will lead to a new world of unity and world law.[26]

FOUR

The Order and Its Master Plan

And we know that we are of God, and the whole world lieth in wickedness.

(1 John 5:19)

We have it in our power to begin the world over again.

Thomas Payne, quoted in
Solar Man

"**S**tep-by-step and stage-by-stage, humanity is achieving oneness. Each day that passes brings some new insight or event which shows conclusively that The Plan is working out. Today, The Plan unfolds at an unprecedented rate bringing all gradually to the envisioned goal." These were said by Benjamin Creme to be the words of the Master, the Lord Maitreya, claimed to be the coming "Christ" for the New Age. According to Creme, a fundamental "change engulfs the world." Creme further maintains that it is The Order, which he calls the Brotherhood, that is responsible for these changes:

The task of the watching Brotherhood is to oversee these changes and contain them lawfully within the confines of

The Plan. Thus, do the Masters work, relating The Plan to the possibilities presented by men.[1]

When Creme refers to "the possibilities presented by man," what he is talking about are crises caused by The Order which, once in progress, present delightful opportunities for The Order to intervene and thus shape the world in the manner called for by The Plan.

Money is the Great Motivator

It is important to understand that the men who run The Order do have a *Plan*. It is also important for us to know that the hidden powers that control this world are motivated in achieving their Plan by the greatest motivator of all time--*money*. The Bible tells us straightforwardly that "the love of money is the root of all evil" (I Timothy 6:10).

The men who plot to rule the world do so to fulfill their lust for money. Greed drives them on. In their consuming hunger to be the richest, and the most powerful men on earth, they will freely use whatever unethical or brutal and vicious acts are necessary.

In the Book of *James* we find that in the last days it will indeed be money that drives the men who would rule the world onto their final destiny. As James prophesied, God's judgement will fall on these men because of their rejection of Christ and their love of the material things of this world which their master lyingly promises them.

Go to now, ye rich men, weep and howl for your miseries that shall come upon you. Your riches are corrupted, and your garments are motheaten. Your gold and silver is cankered; and the rust of them shall be a witness against you, and shall eat your flesh as it were fire. Ye have heaped treasure together *for the last days* (James 5:1-3).

James further tells us that these rich men have "lived in pleasure on the earth, and been wanton." He says that they have "condemned and killed the just; and he doth not resist you." (James 5:5, 6)

We see then that in the last days the rich will obtain their money by "fraud" (James 5:4): they will decadently live in pleasure and they will put to death those who are just. Yet, they will not be resisted by those whom they slay, says James.

It is significant that the gold and silver that these men collect shall be a witness against them. As Jesus so wisely stated, it is easier for a camel to go through the eye of a needle than for a rich man to enter into the Kingdom of God. God is looking for the humble and the meek, for those who debase themselves. But the men of The Order are the arrogant, the bold, the defiant and rebellious. They are far from humble, they are prideful and desirous of gain.

The whole world is the field of harvest for these rich men. Yet, they do not themselves labor, but wrongly use the laborer to bring in the harvest and then they refuse to share with him. Moreover, all that they do is by design. In the dark, reprobate recesses of their minds they have conceived a Plan.

I demonstrated very clearly in my book *Dark Secrets of The New Age* that The Plan exists. Yes, the small, greedy society of money-minded leeches have a Plan for world domination and this Plan is being worked out across the globe. It is a Plan that will result in a new spirituality, a Plan that will destroy the U.S. dollar and wreck the American economy. This Plan will result in a One World Order--indeed, this is one goal that is at the very threshold of attainment--and it will result in total dictatorial control by the elite members of The Order.

Do not think that you can escape this insidious Plan by any means that you can devise with your worldly mind. There is only one route of escape from these madmen that would rule the world. That escape is through the precious blood of Jesus Christ, the Lamb of God slain from the foundation of the world. In a sense, God offers us a helicopter that we can ride on the way out. True, we may be subject to buffeting, to stress, and even to extreme persecution by this group and their secret design. But always, we should remember the words of Jesus when He told us that we should not fear him who could destroy the body, but fear only He who could destroy the soul for eternity. The only one who can do that, of course, is God Himself.

Proof that The Plan exists is so conclusive and there is so much evidence available that I could probably spend two or three hundred pages of this book exploring that documentation alone. I do not wish to do so. There are more important things to discuss. I will, however, provide you a few elements of proof to underscore for readers that The Plan does exist.

The Plan

Vera Stanley Alder, a British elitist who has written many books about this Plan, has assured her many readers that The Plan does in fact exist. "There is actually a Plan," she says. It's aims include the establishment of "a World Organization...a World Economy...a World Religion."[2]

John Randolph Price, reigning leader of the Planetary Commission, also writes of The Plan:

> The Divine Plan is the Strategy and the Blueprint for each individual man or woman, for the entire human race, and for the planet itself, as conceived by...the Will of God.[3]

What we must understand is that when John Randolph Price speaks of "God," he is not talking about the personal God of the Bible. Again we see the god of the New Age, a nebulous god of forces. In essence, all of humanity is collectively "god" according to The Order and its pagan doctrine. Thus, it is the will of the *superman*, the elite of The Order, that has designed the Plan. The real truth, of course, is that the Plan is designed by masters of the Adversary who silently work and plot from their celestial realm, which we know simply as the pit.

A high-ranking diplomat who has often spoken of The Plan is Robert Muller, former Assistant Secretary General of the United Nations and presently Chancellor of the Peace University in San Jose, Costa Rica. Muller speaks in rapturous tones as he declares this Plan to be evolutionary in nature and "glorious and beautiful like Aphrodite emerging from the sea."[4]

The Oath of The World Religion

From my research of The Order, it is obvious that each high-ranking member of The Order has made a blood pact with the devil himself. In the New Age Movement we see the seeds and the nucleus of the secret doctrine of a coming world religion that will be offered us by The Order. Someday this world religion will require all on earth to take an oath. Already in the New Age this oath, a statement of affirmation, is being used although very few who are using it truly understand the hideous nature of the commitment they are making.

For example, at the Unity Church of Dallas not too long ago, seminars were conducted entitled "The Master Mind Principle." Participants were told they must take "seven steps into the Master Mind consciousness." Here is the pledge and oath required of the participants:

> I make a decision to place myself completely under the influence and direction of the Master Mind. I ask the Master Mind to take complete charge of my life ....[5]

How frightening to realize that across the world tens of thousands are taking a similar oath. It is the same oath that the men of The Order have made as the guiding light for their life and work.

The Coming of Solar Man

Possibly the best description of The Plan in terms of its call for a One World Government is found in a book generally unavailable to the public through bookstores but distributed widely among members of The Order, entitled *Solar Man.* Authored by Thomas P. Ehrenzeller, this impassioned treatise predicts the coming of "Solar Man," a sort of superbeing who will preside over a world of unparalleled prosperity and peace.

Ehrenzeller carefully describes how the world is to be grouped together in regions with the European Community being the cornerstone of the world government. Ehrenzeller, who at the time of authoring *Solar Man* sat on the national board of directors of the World Federalist Association, had his book published under the auspices of a publishing house that used the name *Apollo Books* and supposedly is headquartered in a small town in Minnesota. Apollo was the great sun god of the Greeks, and since The Order believes in the concept of a "Thousand Points of Light," a network of light which emanates from the Sun God (Lucifer), it is obvious why the name Apollo is used.

In his revealing book, Ehrenzeller quotes Thomas Payne who once announced, "We have it in our power to begin the world over again."[6] What we need to begin anew, says Ehrenzeller, is "a New World System,"[7] "If the leaders in power cannot see the New Age coming, if they cannot help progress, but rather impede it, then the peoples of the world will seek out new leaders."[8] What the author is really implying here, of course, is that The

Order, representing the peoples of the world, will establish new leaders who *will* comply with their directives.

Ehrenzeller talks about a *cleansing* that is needed on earth. According to him, "What we see is the final, most critical stage in the maturation and civilization of man. A great human civilization is to be built."[9] He goes on to declare, "There can be a New World Order."[10]

Pointing out the dangers of nuclear war, Ehrenzeller says that "people are starting to realize that the old systems cannot hope to cope with the crisis of the present... therefore we will save the world by making of it a bright New Age."[11] And how is this to be accomplished? According to Ehrenzeller:

> We will do this by creating regional groups of nations. The different nations can become more compatible. Then, we can form our nations into regional groupings, and we can align those groupings into one unit which can ultimately encompass the entire world. We must form a kind of solidarity . . . and a kind of unity of purpose that the whole of humanity has never yet known.[12]

Through this solidarity of unity of purpose, Ehrenzeller proclaims, the world will reap the vista of "the dawn of the Solar Age."[13] Moreover, he adds, "it will herald the coming of a new *Solar Race* which will last for centuries, millennia even."[14]

Here again we see the belief of The Order in a false god who assumes the name of the Sun deity, but in actuality is none other than Lucifer. He is the pretender who masquerades as "the light of this world." And the many members of The Order networking around the world are the fabled "a Thousand Points of Light," as Freemasonry loves to refer to them. How revealing, then, the statement made again and again by President George Bush, a high-level Mason and a member of other secret globalist societies, that his goal as chief executive is to encourage and promote "a Thousand Points of Light" across America.

As one devotee of the new world to come has written, "By the year 2000 ... the White House will be turned into a Light House. Rays of light will emanate from Washington."[15] This gentleman is only partially right. The rays may emanate from Washington but it is not Washington that is their primary source. The primary source is Lucifer, whom occultists universally venerate as the "father of light." No wonder the apostle Paul warned that Satan often comes to us disguised as an "Angel of Light" and his demon spirits as "ministers of righteousness" (II Corinthians 11:14).

The Solar Age of the World Federalists and the Aquarian Age and New Age of the occultists are all one and the same. The Order would have us believe that the astrological age of Pisces is ending and a new Aquarian Age is in order. Foster Bailey, one of the movers of the Lucis Trust and a man who has been a staunch supporter of occult Freemasonry, has said:

> Yes, our civilization is dying. Let us move on into the new day and begin now to build a new civilization of the Aquarian Age ... The torch of light has been passed to us. The death of our present civilization is inevitable ... A world crisis will hasten its passing which is all to the good. The old civilization must give way to the new ... The new Aquarian Age has this power. Nothing can stop it.[16]

A Multitude of Plans Within Plans

When we speak of *The Plan* which The Order is now carrying out, we should keep in mind that there are many different plans being utilized by the various parts of the overall network. But all are controlled ultimately behind the scenes by The Order. Each cog and chain of the conspiracy has its own unique plan and all fit together.

The Order is responsible for the overall Master Plan because its members directly report to the Master Mind who is its original creator. The many organizations and groups subordinate to the managing board of The Order each carry out their own assigned plan so that there is a coordinated and cohesive effort throughout the vast empire and network.

The Six Goals of The Order

The Plan envisions the attainment of six specific goals by The Order. These goals involve both spiritual and material objectives. Listed below are these six goals, after which I will elaborate briefly on each.

Goal 1. The establishment of a New International Economic Order, unified and under the direct command of the unelected elite on the highest-level board of The Order.

Goal 2. The establishment of what will appear to be a Democratic One World Government, which will actually be controlled behind-the-scenes by The Order.

Goal 3. The conquest and subjugation by economic, financial, and spiritual means of the two superpowers--the United States of America (U.S.A.) and Russia, also known as the Union of Soviet Socialist Republics (U.S.S.R.).

Goal 4. The ascension of the coming United States of Europe as the dominant nation in a confederated One World Government.

Goal 5. The ushering in of a Supreme World Leader to preside over this new, unified One World Government.

Goal 6. The establishment of a One World Religion, which will coordinate all the world's religions, cults, faith groups, and spiritual beliefs under the guidance of a Supreme Pontiff, the spiritual equivalent of the Supreme World Leader.

Toward A Democratic One World Government

It is the aim of The Order to establish a Democratic One World Government. Now if it seems a strange thing to claim a democratic system when, in reality, an oligarchy at the top is in control and rigidly so, you must understand the extraordinary terminology that is used by The Order. You see, to The Order, peace means war, and war means peace. Democracy means totalitarianism, and vice versa. The Order uses a system of double-think, and a special language known as double-speak.

Just as the Communist Constitution of the Soviet Union theoretically guarantees in writing freedom, liberty, and certain other basic inalienable rights to the people as well as the blessings of a democratic system, so too does The Order assure the world of a coming great democratic movement. However, once their supreme leader is fully entrenched in office, the only freedoms allowed by this group will be the "freedom" to worship their master, and to make money if one is a member of the chosen race of superbeings.

The Order has in mind dividing the world into ten regions, or ten spheres of influence. Each of these regions will be an association of nations grouped together according to geography. But above and beyond these ten regions will be three divisions. That is, the whole world is to be divided and placed under the control of three reigning nation-states. The first will be Japan, the second, Europe, and the third a combined U.S.A. and Russia.

This trilateral division is almost exactly what one of

The Order's leading front organizations, the Trilateral Commission, is proposing with only a minor exception. In a revealing interview in the *Christian Science Monitor,* Dr. C. Fred Bergsten, a prominent member of the Trilateral Commission, talked about the plan for a "multi-polar global economy." Dr. Bergsten said that in the coming World Order there will be "management by committee." That committee, he explained, would be made up of experts from North America, Western Europe, and Japan.

Bergsten also talked about the coordination of such financial entities as the World Bank, The International Monetary Fund, and the General Agreement on Tariffs and Trade. And he stated that the U.S.S.R. would be welcomed into the new World Order.[17] We can expect that the Trilateral Commission will more and more discuss the future role of the Soviet Union in this trilateral arrangement. The goal is to merge the U.S.A. and Russia into one economic and social entity.

Europe and Japan to be Exalted

Now the amazing thing is that The Order wishes to exalt Japan, as leader of Asia, and Germany--Germany being the managing partner of the coming United States of Europe now planned tentatively for 1992. *These are the same two world powers that plunged the world into bloodshed and death in the flames of World War II.*

It was the religion of demonic-led emperor worship and ancestral spirit communication in Japan which inspired that oriental power to attempt to dominate Asia and caused Tokyo's Navy to destroy the American naval forces at Pearl Harbor on December 7, 1941. At the same time, Adolf Hitler had put together his storm troopers and his Gestapo, and his generals were leading the

German forces in a deadly march across Western Europe and North Africa and into the frozen steppes of Russia.

Since World War II, of course, both Japan and Germany have behaved. Indeed, while the U.S. and Russia bankrupted their economies in an expensive, frenetic, incredible arms race, Japan and Germany calmly used their industrial resources and money to become premier economic powers. If The Order has its way, *they will become the two greatest economic powerhouses on earth by the year 2000.*

Hitler conceived of Germany and Japan as spiritual soul-mates, members of the exalted Aryan and Atlantian races respectively. This bizarre idea originated from Hitler's study of the *secret doctrine*, babblings and writings from the twisted imagination of Helena Blavatsky, who founded the Theosophy cult in the late 19th century. More on Hitler's madness and his ideas of a superior race later.

America and Russia Are Mongrel Nations

In the view of The Order, both the U.S.A. and Russia are for the most part *mongrel nations*. Each are federations of a diverse number of peoples. They are not of pure blood. This concept of racial purity was not new to Hitler and today it is held not only by some members of the royalty and secret societies in Europe, but also by many of the upper class in Japan.

This heinous racial doctrine still prevailing among the elite in Japan came to light and shocked many of the readers of the *Wall Street Journal* when in that newspaper read by America's financial elite, Toshio Soejima, head of Japan's largest telecommunications firm--indeed *the world's largest*--Nippon T & T Corporation, was quoted as saying:

The Japanese are a people that can manufacture a product of uniformity and superior quality because the Japanese are a race of completely pure blood, not a mongrelized race as in the United States.[18]

This blatantly prejudiced comment from one of Japan's leading industrialists astonished Western observers. Subsequently, Kenchi Takemura, one of Japan's most famous television news reporters, admitted that this attitude is prevalent among some in his country. "The Japanese do not consider others human beings. We tend to be insensitive to things not Japanese."[19]

The United States and the Soviet Union, according to The Order, are made up of a number of nationalities, most of which have intermarried and intermixed. Thus, Hitler maintained that after he had defeated Russia in World War II, he would reduce that nation to a serf state. After killing off most of the Russian citizens, history records that Hitler's plan was to take the Russians who remained and use them as slave laborers good only to provide agricultural products for the German Reich.

This is also the plan of The Order in regards to the United States of America. In their minds we are good farmers and soldiers but inferior in most other respects. In fact, The Order realizes that America has one of the greatest agricultural production rates in the world today. In the radiant New Age, therefore, we will become the bread basket.

To a lesser extent, Russia will be. Of course at present, Russia cannot provide enough food even for itself, but all of this will be taken care of, according to the guidelines of The Plan, as soon as the One World Order gains complete authoritarian control. Then there will be a purification and cleansing action so that the population of Russia will be reduced significantly. For the most part, only those who work the land will survive this purification process.

In America, the same is true. After the misfits are done away with, then there will not be so many mouths to feed and resources can be distributed to those "more" deserving.

Americans and Russians to Become World Policemen

Another role for U.S.A./Russia will be as *world policemen.* Since the "mongrel races" in these countries are brutes who are quite good at exercising military power--witness the fact that both the United States and the Soviet Union have long been famed for their military prowess--it is planned that in the future One World Order, we will become the world policemen for The Order. The U.S.A. and Russia will give their youth as blood sacrifices to enforce global peace and put down rebellions to keep the Lords of Money in office.

A model action was the United States buildup in the Persian Gulf after Saddam Hussein invaded and conquered tiny Kuwait. Here we see the pattern for the future: The United States (and also Russia as need be) sending in *mercenary forces* while the strongest economic powers on planet earth, Japan and Germany, as well as other associated nations in Europe and Asia, for the most part sit idly by.

The military buildup in the Middle East cost America approximately $1.2 billion per month. In addition, it was the U.S. servicemen and women whose lives were on the line, not the Japanese and the Europeans. When war comes, and it will come in order to enforce the New Order, it will be the serf states of the U.S.A. and Russia, owned as they are by the Japanese and European juggernauts, who pay the bitter price.

It is interesting to note that in George Orwell's *1984,* there is also a trilateral division of world powers, and war was a major preoccupation of these powers. Could it be that George Orwell knew, even in 1948 at the time his monumental and frightening book was first published, that The Order was alive and well? Did Orwell know of their plans?

It should also be noted that if Israel does not behave, or perhaps even if it does, at some future juncture the United States and Russia will be ordered by the elite to put down the Jewish state. This could very well fulfill Bible prophecy. We read in Ezekiel 38 and 39 that in the last days the great nation to the *utter north* of the nation of Israel (Russia, as can easily be seen on any map) will invade Israel along with a number of other nations (including *Gomer*, or Germany) that are named. The Order's use of the U.S.A./Russia trilateral group of nations could prove very prophetic.

Social and Spiritual Transformation in the U.S.A. and Russia

A major emphasis of the Order and its many front organizations--especially those that are church-related-- has been to radically alter the spiritual and moral belief systems of both the United States and the Soviet Union. The growth of the New Age Movement and the increasing immorality in all walks of American life are indicators of just how successful this effort has been. The ultimate objective is an entirely new spirituality.

In the Soviet Union emphasis has been on re-establishing *spirituality* as the era of atheism ends. The newfound spirituality will be based on occultism, old Russian and ethnic paganism, and New Age innovations. While traditional, Biblical Christianity is now also gaining adherents in Russia, the masters of that country will be doing their best to channel spiritual interests toward a more preferred type of apostate, pagan "Christianity."

The Order fully realizes that a form of New Age/pagan spirituality is more perfectly compatible with its aims.

The Fourth Reich Of The Super-rich

According to one of its chief goals, The Order intends to create a United States of Europe. At the helm of this powerful confederation of nations will be a unified Germany. The United States of Europe will become the seat of world government and it will be from its capitol that the supreme World Leader will reign.

In the following chapter we will examine the role of the coming World Leader and discover the ingenius methods and strategies he plans to use to achieve the six major goals of the conspiracy.

FIVE

A World Leader for the New Millennium

Let no man deceive you by any means: for that day shall not come, except there come a falling away first, and that man of sin be revealed, the son of perdition; Who opposeth and exalteth himself above all that is called God, or that is worshipped; so that he as God sitteth in the temple of God, shewing himself that he is God.

(II Thessalonians 2:3-4)

Send us a man, whether he be God or the devil, and we will receive him.

Henri Spaak,
Secretary-General of NATO

Goal number 3 of the Plan is the crowning of their own chosen one to be the supreme *World Leader*. This will fulfill Revelation 13 which describes a beast that rises out of the sea. This beast, known by Christians as the Antichrist and designated with the number 666, will be widely admired as great statesman and diplomat. He will rule with the advice and consent of The Order.

Today, in leadership positions around the world, there are already men appointed by The Order not because of merit, but simply due to heritage. Their father and grandfathers before them received favored son treatment. These are the blue bloods, the multi-generational race of supposed supermen.

It will be the task of the World Leader to see to the extermination of the inferior races. It will also be the task of the World Leader to see to it that the world's money supply is securely under the watchful eye of The Order. The World Leader will therefore be a man of consummate financial skills. He will be a wizard of the financial marketplace and will know how to consolidate banking operations around the world and centralize their management. Central financial planning is a key element in order to fulfill the plans of The Order.

Money to be Major Concern of World Leader

In her book *Externalization of the Hierarchy*, the high priestess of the New Order, the late Alice Bailey, explains that the acquisition, possession, and management of money will be the major concern of the coming World Leader:

> When the *adjuster of finances* (as an advanced disciple from this Ashram is called in the Hierarchy) appears, he will find conditions greatly changed from those now prevalent and this to the following extent: #1. The principle of barter and exchange (to the benefit of all concerned) will control. #2. National currencies will have been largely superceded, not only by a system of barter but by a universal monetary exchange...[1]

This system of barter exchange is confirmed as essential by Vera Stanley Alder. She carefully prescribes a system to be set up whereby there will be a Council For Economics that reports to the President of Earth, also known simply as the World Leader. According to Alder, "the principles of world government . . . should insist on the right of every man to the necessities of life, the best available chances of education, and the possibility of cultivating his own piece of land."[2] She says that the Council For Economics would see to the just redistribution of resources so that all will be shared in common.

This is, of course, a bunch of socialistic nonsense, but socialism is exactly what is prescribed by The Order. As we continue to read of Alder's blueprint for the money system we see her dictum that "money will come to be considered as crystallized power or spiritual energy." She adds: "Therefore, its manipulation will become a solemn responsibility, closely under the guidance of the spiritual council."[3]

Alder also describes the coming cashless society:

> Economics will be founded on a quite different basis from that of the present capitalistic system. A system of exchange between peoples of goods and services will, when intelligently developed, gradually cancel out the need for buying and selling with money.[4]

All Food, Gold, and Silver to be Owned by State

If Alder's detailed blueprint is carried out by The Order, *food* will be closely controlled by a World Food Authority, and *gold, silver, and other precious metals* would be seized from individual owners. A *universal currency* would also be issued and a *new marking and identification system* used for purchases made:

> Agricultural surpluses will be passed through a "Central Surplus Pool," controlled by the Council For Economics. There would be no need for a paper currency, nor even for

the retention of gold, silver, and other precious metals by individuals or countries. Money as such would revert to its original token value. As the bulk of commerce would be carried on by the means of exchange, and individual needs would be supplied on a ration card system, the need for the handling of money would dwindle.

There will of course be a universal currency the world over. There would be a central bank which decided the value or price cheaply in terms of labor and quality of all goods produced. This value would probably be described in terms of letters and numbers, the letters representing the quality of work in material and the numbers representing the hours of work entailed."[5]

The system described by Alder to be instituted by the coming World Leader and his associates will fulfill to the very letter Revelation 13:17: "And that no man might buy or sell, save he that had the mark, or the name of the beast, or the number of his name."

The proposed system will give a value for each purchase "in terms of letters and numbers." This is chilling, as is the intention to institute a ration card system. If this system is ever adopted, the reign of the coming "President of Earth" will be hellish indeed.

It is equally scary to read Alder's dark comments in her chapter "From Self-Mastery to World Service." She proclaims that the supreme goal of the coming World Order will be to achieve the "oneness and the interdependence of humanity," with its motto being *The greatest good for the greatest number.*[6]

In other words, *individual rights* will be stamped out as the elite decides what is in the best interest of *all humanity.* Alder's sly use of the phrase, "The greatest good for the greatest number," is the same slogan and motto used by the Lucis Trust, the Tara Center, World Goodwill, and many other front organizations set up by The Order.

The Imperialistic Conquest of The United States And Soviet Russia

To create a trilateral world of three power centers, Japan, Europe, and U.S.A./Russia, it is necessary that the World Leader whittle the U.S.A. and Russia down to size. Until the decade of the 70s, the United States was the greatest economic powerhouse in the world. Its balance of trade showed surpluses, the dollar was strong, and this nation occupied a position of preeminence in the world. No longer is this true. There have been subversive forces at work in the United States and abroad first to equalize the United States' economy in comparison with Germany, Japan and others overseas, and then finally to force America to sink ever downward to become a second-rate economic power.

The same is true of Soviet Russia, although in that country The Order got a lot of help from the rulers in the Kremlin with their ill-conceived policies of socialism and collectivism and their arrogant goal of world domination and military supremacy.

The Order's decision that Europe, led by Germany, and Japan are to be the two key financial leaders in the New International Economic Order and that U.S.A./Russia will play a subordinate role as world food producer and policeman has produced striking economic results over the past few decades. The long term policy of the megabanks controlled by The Order has been to slowly strangle and throttle America economically. Though it has taken many years to accomplish, this project has been eminently successful.

We are finally seeing the final stages of what I call the "Great Sell-off and Looting of America." Germany, Britain and other nations in the European community, and Japan, Korea, Taiwan, and others in Asia, have bought controlling interest in American corporations. They also now own much of the prime real estate in major cities and markets throughout the continental United States.

Why are our leaders allowing this economic catastrophe to occur? Why do they let us be strangled? We can see in their public statements that the spokespersons for such groups as the Trilateral Commission, the Council on Foreign Relations, and the Sovereign Military Order of Malta have no true loyalty and patriotism to their native nation, the U.S.A. Instead, infiltrating at all levels of government and industry, they have used their money and positions to destroy the American economy and to transfer American wealth to foreigners, especially to their colleagues in Germany and Japan.

Moreover, the American genius for invention and originality has been abused by such nations as Japan. After Americans come up with original ideas for everything from lasers to computers and for all types of electronic devices and instruments--from television sets and electric toasters to microwave ovens and new communication networks-- the imitators in Japan go to work with their copycat models.

To their credit, their scientists have often improved upon the basic American models. But research and development costs are staggering, and often, after American entrepreneurs have spent millions or even billions to invent and produce certain products, the Japanese make slight improvements and then move rapidly to take over the world market. In effect, they have stolen the American patents. In this way, America has become more and more impoverished as its goods are rejected in the world marketplace.

Bureaucrats Aid the Economic Takeover of America

To assist the coming World Leader, The Order has also been able to install political leaders at the top echelons of America's government, especially in what is called the fourth branch of government, the bureaucracy. It is the bureaucrats at the Department of State, Department of Commerce, Department of Treasury, the Justice Department, and the numerous agencies that regulate international trade that are crammed full of CFR, TLC, and Lucis Trust members who use their influence to build up such nations as Germany and Japan while diminishing the success of American trade efforts.

The Coming Great Economic Depression

All the evidence indicates that without a doubt the manipulators have in the wings a Great Depression for America (and Canada). It will be an economic downswing so severe that it will startle the citizens of this nation and drive America directly into the arms of the waiting members of the One World Order.

When financial crisis and panic grips Americans, when unemployment flies up to 20 percent or more and a 1990s repeat of the 1929 stock market crash is blasted all over the news networks, The Order believes the American public will cry out for its leadership to do something. Anything. Then those leaders of The Order who have carefully and gradually over the years wormed their way into top positions of leadership in the American government will simply sign over to the European Community and the Japanese deed and title to all the treasure houses of this once great continent.

Soviet Bear Declawed

The Soviet Bear has also been declawed by The Order. Stalin complained about being encircled. Although the monstrous policies of Stalin and his butchering of at least 25 million of his own people certainly cause us to falter in our sympathy, we know for a fact that Russia was indeed encircled economically. In fact, it was George Kennan, a member of the CFR, who in the 1950s fine-tuned a policy which the West called the "Containment" of Russia.

This Containment over the ensuing decades finally has resulted in the almost total economic and financial collapse of the communist titan. Of course, the idiocy of the communists and their dogged refusal to let go of their unrealistic goal of world domination was a great boost to the cause of The Order. Judgment seems to have finally arrived for the leaders of this godless, atheistic nation-state.

Today, President Gorbachev regularly visits the capitals of Bonn, London, Rome, Paris, and Washington, D.C., begging to join the coming United States of Europe. He is saying almost on bended knees, "Please let us join the Common European Home. Please let us enter the door to prosperity." So far, The Order has turned Gorbachev down cold, although there have been some crumbs shoved his way. In exchange for Gorbachev's bringing Eastern Europe and the Soviet Union into the sphere of influence of The Order, and in exchange for his softening of the role of world communism, The Order has agreed to increase trade between the Soviet bloc, the European Community, the United States, and others and has promised to help the Soviet Union out by providing high tech equipment and new, improved industrial machinery.

For example, according to news accounts, in exchange for Russia allowing Germany to reunite, Chancellor Helmut Kohl of West Germany guaranteed to provide the Kremlin grants and loans of up to $15 billion. This is a shot in the arm for the Russian economy which is now in a most desperate strait. Gorbachev has also been guaranteed favored trading status by The Order and he has been told that the ruble will be integrated into the coming world currency system.

As long as Russia behaves itself and Gorbachev or his successors do what The Order tells them to do, the Soviets will continue to be thrown crumbs off the table. For now, the Russians have no choice but to accede to the demands of The Order. The masters of the Kremlin realize full well that their people are in a surly state of rebellion and mutiny because of the great shortages of consumer goods and the pitiful state of the Russian economy.

The Arms Race Has Hurt America's Economy

It should be noted, too, that The Order has been thrilled at the great arms race and its devastating effect over the years on both the U.S.A. and Russia. While Germany and Japan sat back in the lap of luxury and devoted their financial resources to building at breakneck speed a tremendously strong civilian industrial empire, the United States and Russia threw hundreds of billions of dollars down the drain, developing, producing and putting on-line expensive tactical and strategic weapon systems.

Now, given the post-Cold War situation, conventional forces are primarily what is needed to serve as a world police force. Strategic weaponry, in particular ICBM's, cruise missiles, Star Wars platforms, nuclear missile carrying submarines, and other high cost systems, are proving to be albatrosses. The use of conventional military power is most needed in the small brush fire conflicts most likely to occur around the world. Therefore, these expensive systems now in the possession of the United States and the Soviet Union may well become relics of a faded and now bygone era. Increasingly, the eagle and the bear are becoming antiquated, pitiful warriors, in a new world in which economic forces dictate which nations have the most power.

The Economic Cold War is Over--They Won!

In essence, what the masters of Germany and Japan were unable to do in World War II by bullets and bombs, they have been able to accomplish since that time with their marks and yen. After decades of assault their imperialistic conquest of the United States and the Soviet Union is almost complete. Perhaps it is significant to remember that at the end of World War II, Japan's god-man emperor, Hirohito, refused to use the term *surrender*. The Empire of the Rising Sun, said the emperor, had merely decided to "stop fighting."[7]

The reported last words of Hitler also jar the mind. Aware of the magnitude of his overwhelming defeat by the allied powers, and having decided to kill himself and have his mate, Eva Braun, commit suicide, rather than be taken captive by the Americans and the Russians, a dejected but still defiant Hitler declared:

> It is necessary that I should die for my people; but my spirit will rise from the grave and the world will know that I was right.[8]

Will the demon spirit that possessed Hitler also possess the coming World Leader of the Fourth Reich of the super-rich? Bible prophecy indicates that Satan himself may indwell this vile person (see II Thessalonians 2). He will be a much greater personality than Hitler!

Amazingly, some years ago, in 1957, Henri Spaak, then Secretary-General of NATO in Europe, told an audience, "We are tired of Committees. Send us a *man* whether he be *God* or the *devil* and we will receive him."

The Rise of the False Prophet

While five of the six goals of The Order are concerned with accomplishing political and economic objectives, the sixth, equally important, involves *spiritual objectives*. It is the intent of The Order that there be *two men* at the helm of global leadership. One man, the *World Leader*, will guide the destinies of the nations, controlling the political order and the economic structures of the nation-state system within its trilateral groupings.

The second man at the top, subservient to the World Leader but powerful in his own right, will be the *Spiritual Overseer* of all the world's people. He will be the one who causes the world's religions and faith groupings to focus their eyes on and throw their full support and endorsement behind the World Leader and The Plan of The Order. Bible prophecy describes this man as the "False Prophet" (Revelation 19:20).

Now, although the elitist members of The Order secretly practice a religion based on Luciferian doctrines, for practical reasons and expediency they encourage a religious philosophy based on the universal concept of "God as you understand him." The New World Religion and its spiritual helmsman will not support any one religious system or set of dogma. Instead, all religions, all beliefs, all religious practices are to be adjudged of equal worth and value. Whatsoever god or gods men and women choose to serve is of no consequence, as long as they do serve a deity of sorts.

Another cardinal rule is that whatever religion or faith to which a person ascribes, the individual must go along with a doctrine of tolerance and *unconditional acceptance* of all other faith systems. In the bright new future, it will be acceptable to believe in anyone and anything as long as one does not advocate exclusivity.

The infamous British satanist, Aleister Crowley, still widely regarded as a great spiritual presence by the men of The Order, set forth in his writings the one great commandment of The Order. Still accepted today as the greatest of all commandments by New Agers, witches, and, occultists, it is simply this: "Do what thou wilt shall be the whole of the law." This is, Crowley taught, the "Word" of the New Age.[9]

The Supreme Law of the Masons

Freemasonry, the fraternity shared by those in The Order, accepts this unholy commandment. In his revealing treatise, *Emergence of The Mystical*, Henry C. Clausen, 33rd degree, and formerly Sovereign Grand Commander of the Supreme Council of the Ancient and Accepted Scottish Rite of Freemasonry (the Mother Supreme Council of the World for Freemasons), offered this wisdom to Masons throughout the planet:

> Each man is his own absolute law giver, the dispenser of glory or gloom to himself; the decreer of his life, his reward, his punishment.[10]

This law of the Masons and The Order directly conflicts with the Word of God. In Proverbs 28:26 we read: "He that trusteth in his own heart is a fool..."

We see, then, that the universal religion advocated by The Order and required of all of its subjects will be the humanistic, self-centered philosophy of the New Age movement. In fact, this will be a New Age World Religion, a uniting of all world religions into one. Protestant, Catholic, Hindu, Buddhist, African tribal worship, native American Indian--it does not matter in the New Age. All are one.

Believers in A Personal God Not Welcome

However, there are at least *three groups* which will not be allowed to exist in this coming world religious system: *fundamentalist Christians, orthodox Jews,* and *fundamentalist Moslems.* Each of these groups refuses to yield and merge its body of beliefs with the other world religions. Each claims itself to be exclusive. Moreover, the fundamentalist Christians and Moslems and the orthodox Jews commonly believe in a personal God, whereas The Order, in its propaganda for the masses, claims that there is no personal God, only a god of energy forces, a nebulous and impersonal divine intelligence. Thus, true Christianity, Judaism, and Islam are incompatible with the goals of The Order.

So we can expect hard times for those who practice such religions and especially for Christians. Christians are continually a thorn in the side of The Order because of the intervention of the Holy Spirit on their behalf.

A world religion sponsored by The Order will also affirm belief that the nebulous god of forces may come in any shape or fashion. It can be a he or a she. Indeed, *goddess worship* will be the principle form of veneration of deity in the new world religion. The pagan gods and goddesses of India, the orient, and ancient Babylon, Rome, Greece, and the Celts will increasingly find favor in the coming new world.

Will The Vatican Become World Religion Headquarters?

Though many Catholics will no doubt become very alarmed over the prospect, it is clearly factual that The Order desires that the Vatican be the fount and the headquarters of the New World Religion and intends that the Pope of the Roman Catholic Church become the

Supreme Pontiff of the whole world. The pope is to
become the earth's King/Priest. He is to marshal the spiritual resources of the planet. He will also proclaim that all
religions are one and that "God" has given divine
authority, absolute rights, and responsibility to the World
Leader.

Already the Pope is viewed as the world's greatest
spiritual leader, by mainline Protestant denominations and
other world religions. Quickly, all are coming together
while the few true Christians who refuse to join this false
unity movement are increasingly being portrayed as hard-
line separatists worthy of scorn and abuse.

It is expected that the pope will instill in peoples a
keen desire to worship the goddess as the Queen of
Heaven. Word will be put out to the faithful of all
religions that Mary is an archetype of all the goddesses of
the past, from Isis in Egypt, Ishtar in Babylon and
Ashtoreth in ancient Israel, to Venus in Rome and Athena
and Diana in Greece. "Mary" and the other goddesses will
all be seen to be one and the same. It will also be pro-
mulgated that it does not matter which goddess you pray
to or petition since all their spiritual energies emanate
from the same source. All are to be viewed as intercessors
between man and "God."

The pope will also espouse the philosophy that the
Great Spiritual Sun is sending to earth many rays of light
and this is why there are many world religions. Each man
and woman, so the claim will go, may follow the light of
his or her own choosing. All men will be seen as brothers
and as members of the global community. The belief that
Jesus is *the* Way, *the* Truth, *the* Life will be declared
obsolete, bigoted and narrow-minded, and unloving.

When the bleak day arrives that all of the above come
into being, you will know for sure that the return of our
Lord is imminent. Then, the Supreme Pontiff, the
Antichrist World Leader, and the other members of The
Order will know that the game is over. Finished. I pray
that day will come soon.

SIX

Occult Theocracy

*And the ten horns which thou sawest are ten kings,
which have received no kingdom as yet; but receive
power as kings one hour with the beast. These have
one mind, and shall give their strength and power unto
the beast.*

(Revelation 17:12-13)

*In the nuclear age, humanity must evolve a new mode
of political thought, a new concept of the world . . . a
new way of thinking. . . . Revolutions always begin in
the mind . . .*

Mikhail Gorbachev, President, U.S.S.R.
Perestroika

There is a certain man who once each year,
to celebrate the spring equinox, goes up
to the top of a "sacred" mountain in
France. There, he sits in the lotus position so familiar to
the Hindu and Yoga teachers and beats a staccato rhythm
on primitive sticks. His goal is to communicate with the
spirits of the earth.

Now, given the fact that shamans and witchdoctors are
commonplace in today's New Age-infested world, this
event would not ordinarily arouse our curiousity.

However, in this instance, we should definitely sit up and take notice. The man just described as attempting to communicate with the spirit world is a most important individual: his name is *Francois Mitterand*, and he is currently the president of France, a nation which possesses enough nuclear-tipped missiles to destroy much of our globe![1]

Perhaps it should come as no surprise that President Francois Mitterand recently stated that he is not afraid of a reunified Germany, that he in fact thinks a strong Germany is *good* for Europe. Could it be that the same demonic and conspiratorial forces which are shaping Germany and the coming United States of Europe into the "New Rome" are also influencing Monsieur Mitterand?

Shocking as it may seem, there is an occult explosion among today's world leaders. Americans may have been surprised at the revelation by his Chief of Staff Donald Regan that astrologist Joan Quigley guided the minute affairs of state during the eight-year presidency of Ronald Reagan. But this was and is only the tip of the iceberg. Many other revelations and secrets about American and other world leaders lie beneath the surface, awaiting disclosure by courageous men and women in the know.

The Occult Theocracy That Runs the World

The elite in Germany, Great Britain, the U.S.A., France, and elsewhere who run the political and economic affairs of our world are most often not Christians as we might suppose. The evidence clearly establishes that these men-- and the leaders of the secret societies and orders whom they represent--are occultists whose spiritual loyalty is pledged to pagan deities or simply to "The Force."

The Mystical Prince and the Great Global Land Grab

A prime example of the new type of occult political leader is the dashing Prince Charles, heir to the British throne. It is well-documented that the Prince is a believer in the powers of occult symbols; he advocates New Age "holistic" health care, and has dabbled with spirit channeling, astrology, divination by pendulum, the I Ching, and occult visualization.[2]

The Prince, who is already--even before coronation as reigning Monarch--taking an active part in government and society, is also tied in with the conspiratorial Trilateral Commission. Last year Prince Charles addressed members of the Trilateral Commission in London and promoted his and Prince Philip's grandiose plan for a World Conservation Bank.[3]

This plan, whose architects include banker David Rockefeller, U.S. Secretary of State James Baker, Baron de Edmund Rochschild, and other Trilateral and CFR members, would require the U.S. megabanks to "forgive" the multibillion dollar debts owed them by such Third World countries as Brazil and Mexico. In exchange, those countries would sign over legal deeds for millions of acres of undeveloped land to the internationalists. They in turn have set up a fraudulent institution called the World Conservation Bank to hold the title to these valuable lands.[4]

It is anticipated that once the Third World nations have coughed up their land, under threat of being forced into bankruptcy by the big boys if they refuse, then such industrial nations as the United States, Canada, Australia, New Zealand and others will be told that they, too, must sign over their wilderness properties. But not to worry. Prince Charles, the Rockefellers and Rothschilds and the other Lords of Money will take good care of the one-third of the world's resources that are to be handed them on a silver platter.

This scam is now being avidly backed and promoted by

the U.S. Department of the Interior, the Department of the Treasury, the Environmental Protection Agency and other governmental bodies. The pretense is that the elitists simply want to "preserve natural resources." But in reality this scheme could best be described as the Great Global Land Grab.

Voodoo and Devil Worship in Central America

The long arm of the money masters stretches far down south to Latin America, where their lackeys--tin horn dictators and occult politicians--rule the people in an atmosphere of dark occultism.

For example, it is common knowledge among some in Nicaragua that former Marxist Sandinista dictator Daniel Oretega is deeply involved in satanism and witchcraft. Indeed, Ortega's wife in 1989 sponsored and participated in a worldwide witch's convocation held in Nicaragua's capital of Managua.

In 1989 when Panama's military dictator Manuel Antonio Noriega was deposed through an armed invasion by U. S. armed forces, the victors were startled by what they discovered at Noriega's secret hideaway. They found bones, dried chicken blood, black candles, ritual magic texts, and other paraphernalia connected with black magic and voodooism.

It should be noted, too, that Noriega stashed some of his illegal drug-running profits in a Swiss bank and that he had been in the employ of the CIA as an informant. More connections!

Insiders were not surprised when Noriega's occult involvement was revealed. Even prior to the invasion and discovery by U.S. forces, reports were beginning to surface that Noriega was a practicing occultist.

"Psychic Powers are Part of Battle Among Panamanian Rivals," blared a June 20, 1987 New York Times headline.[5] In a remarkable story that reveals exactly where the whole world is headed, Times staffer Stephen Kinzer reported on an internal battle brewing in Panama, home to the strategically located Panama Canal, between strong-man military Gen. Manuel Antonio Noriega and arch-rival Col. Roberto Diaz. The battle was of the occult, with Col. Diaz calling on his New Age guru, a "holy man," Sai Baba from India, to help him ward off hostile negative energies focused at him by General Noriega.

Meanwhile, the New York Times reported, yet a third high-ranking political figure, Dr. Arnulfo Arias Madrid, also was sharpening psychic claws and had joined the fight. According to insiders, Dr. Madrid had devoted his life to the study of the supernatural.

Rev. Javier Villanueva, a Panamanian Roman Catholic priest, explained to the Times that "Diaz, Noriega, and Madrid are all searching for an extra edge in their political struggle. They think that the edge is to be found in the world of spirits and the occult."

A Plague of Occultism

The evidence is mounting that many other world political leaders, statesmen, and diplomats are implicated in occultism through the One World religious and political efforts and philosophies of the secret societies that sustain the New Age Movement. For example, the Planetary Initiative for the World We Choose, a hardcore political group dedicated to globalism, is strongly supported by dignitaries ranging from the Dalai Lama, the exiled spiritual leader of Tibet, to Robert Muller, former Assistant Secretary General of the United Nations. Other members include Rev. Theodore Hesburgh, chancellor of the University of

Notre Dame, famed scientist Linus Pauling, Congressman James Weaver, Catholic priest Robert F. Drinan, Mayor Don Fraser of Minneapolis, writer Norman Cousins, United Nations official Ervin Lazlo, science fiction writer Isaac Asimov, and comedian/actor Steve Allen.

As many as 300 similar groups exist, each working fervently to bring in a One World economic, social, and political order. R. E. "Ted" Turner, chairman of Cable News Network (CNN) and the Turner Broadcasting System, was instrumental in 1987 in setting up one such group, the Better World Society. Turner, who called for the election in 1988 of a New Age president for the U.S.A., is pro-Soviet in view and is a peace at any cost advocate.

Declaring the world a "global village" and insisting that arms reduction treaties be signed between the superpowers, the Better World Society has boldly paid for and funded a number of commercial TV ads inviting citizens to write for more information. When they do, they discover--perhaps to their horror and astonishment--that this awful group proposes to use the media and especially the television system in every country to aggressively promote its decidedly unpatriotic brand of globalism.

Worse, the inquirer discovers that sitting on the organization's board of directors are such luminaries as Jimmy Carter, former president of the United States; Gro Harlem Brundtland, prime minister of Norway; Jacques Cousteau, French marine scientist and environmental activist; Lester Brown, president of the peace-oriented Worldwatch Institute; and Prince Aga Khan, the wealthy Middle East potentate who heads up an international commission on "humanitarian issues."

Satan Goes To Washington

Washington, D.C. is crowded these days with New Age and pro-One World Order politicians and diplomats. Reagan's former Secretary of State George Schultz, for one. He is intimately linked with both the Council on Foreign Relations and the Trilateral Commission. Secretary Schultz presented a speech before the World Affairs Council in early 1988 that clearly established his credentials among the elitists. Proposing that the world had suprisingly and with little fanfare entered a "New Age," Schultz insisted that the world needs to realign its thinking so we can "respond to the new order of things."[6]

This New Order, Secretary Schultz remarked, means new opportunities. But, said Schultz, to take advantage of these opportunities "we must discard outdated habits of thinking and make room for new possibilities." Only then, he suggests, can we "partake of some of the fruits of the New Age." What we must do, Schultz continued, is to "create a more just and decent social order."[7]

That he meant a *One World Order* was unquestionable. In his speech the Secretary of State carefully justified the need for such a One World system. For example, he advocated the creation of a close-knit, financial system by explaining:

The speed at which information flows has already created a global financial market. Markets are no longer places but electronic networks ... They are outstripping the traditional means by which governments deal with them. The amount of money that changes hands in the global financial markets in one day exceeds $1 trillion--more than the entire budget of the U.S. government for a year. Such flows transcend national boundaries and can overwhelm rigid economic policies.[8]

Keep in mind that George Schultz is no ordinary man. At the time he made the above speech, he was Secretary of State of the U.S.A., in charge of foreign affairs for a superpower nation and head of U.S. embassies in 173 countries. George Schultz is, of course, not alone in his New Age views. Congress is also rampant with New Age politicians.

In April, 1985 U.S. Senator Claiborne Pell (Democrat, Rhode Island) gave a tea for members of Congress to honor Jiddu Krishnamurti, an Indian philosopher who was once hand-picked by the occultic Theosophy Society to be possessed by a spirit and become the New Age "Messiah" and "World Teacher." VIPs ranging from famed economist Milton Friedman to a Reagan White House speechwriter and a former special assistant to President Gerald Ford, also met with Krishnamurti (now deceased). Economist Friedman was also able to arrange a major public appearance for Krishnamurti at Washington's Kennedy Center. Krishnamurti's speech topic, predictably, was "Do We Really Want Peace?" though he also managed to get across his New Age/Hindu pitch that "God is an illusion."[9]

I could go on and on, describing, for example, the New Age beliefs of former presidential candidate and Senator Gary Hart, who once told a TV interviewer that he received *daily* spiritual and religious advise from a Native American Indian "princess" and is also reported to frequent Indian sweat lodges. There's U.S. Senator Terry Sanford (Democrat, North Carolina) a member of the World Federalists whose world-view matches that of the New Age globalists right down the line; and there's also Houston Mayor Kathy Whitmire, a New Age heroine, and Minneapolis Mayor Don Fraser, active in the nuclear freeze movement and a supporter of Planetary Citizens.[10]

Chancellors and Queens Join the Globalism/Occultic Bandwagon

Overseas in Europe, we find globalism leader Willy Brandt, former chancellor of West Germany, the highest elective post in that Western European nation. Brandt was instrumental in the issuance of a report of the Socialist International, "The Global Challenge," setting forth what are basically doctrinal New Age goals for world unity and sharing. In Great Britain, Queen Elizabeth is a supporter of New Age humanist and holistic health philosophies while Prince Philip promotes a return to pagan religions. In the Netherlands, Prince Bernhard and Queen Juliana work tirelessly on behalf of the Bilderbergers, the Planetary Initiative for the World We Choose and similar one worldism groups.

Former Secretary-General of the United Nations Kurt Waldheim, now president of Austria, was also active in the New Age movement until his background as a Nazi military officer allegedly responsible for war crimes and atrocities suddenly came to light. He has since curtailed his New Age activities though he continues to play an important role in the world peace movement, a priority item on the conspirators' political agenda.

Regardless of the fact that Waldheim has repeatedly lied about his Nazi past and connections, he was elected president of his native country of Austria by a handy margin of victory. In 1987 Waldheim was warmly greeted by the Pope at the Vatican in Rome as he paid a state visit.

As you can see, Satan has performed miracles in founding and fostering a massive world movement destined to fulfill the prophetic role described in Daniel, Ezekiel, Amos, Thessalonians, Revelation, and other books of the Bible. But without a doubt, *his greatest achievement has been in winning Eastern European and Soviet leaders to the cause.*

Eastern Europe: A Harbinger of Things to Come?

The American TV and press media have bombarded us with positive stories and news features about the break-up of communism in Eastern Europe. The myth, only partially correct, is that democracy will now reign victoriously supreme, that freedom and liberty is assured. Some believe that Christianity will also flourish in these countries.

Certainly we should be hopeful that democratic and especially Christian values will gain ground in Eastern Europe, but our optimism should be tempered. Already there are increasing reports that occultism, Satanism, and New Ageism are in resurgence in Eastern Europe.

For example, in Czechoslovakia, former playwright and now president Vaclav Havel is a New Ager who recently invited the Dalai Lama of Tibetan Buddhism to his country so they could "meditate" together. On a trip to America, Havel addressed a joint session of the U.S. Congress and was wildly applauded; yet, the occultic, one world organization World Goodwill recently commended Havel as a "visionary" who speaks of the need for a "global revolution in the sphere of human consciousness."[11]

Have we traded communism in Eastern Europe for something which will ultimately prove equally harmful and dangerous?

Gorbachev and the Soviet New Age State

Only a few years ago it might have seemed preposterous to describe the Soviet Union as a budding New Age state. But today, we are being presented a spectacle that is unparalleled in either the history of the Soviet Union or the world. The younger, dynamic man in charge of the Kremlin and the Soviet Communist Party, Mikhail Gorbachev, is rapidly steering his vast and powerful nation through the rippling waves of darkness toward New Age shores. Is it possible that comrade Gorbachev is now in the camp of the men who run The Order?

The same *Time* magazine that once lionized Gorbachev as its 1987 "Man of the Year" now reports that their hero is buying into the New Age religion. "Gorby The New Age Guru?" was the recent headline of a feature by *Time* reporter David Ellis. Here's what Ellis had to say about Gorbachev's newfound spirituality:

> Fans of Harmonic Convergences and the like have been noting Mikhail Gorbachev's frequent use of phrases associated with the New Age Movement, that mystical universalist philosophy that preaches--as the Soviet president does--of the need for "A New World Order."

> As Gorbachev said in California, "All mankind is entering a New Age, and world trends are beginning to obey new laws and logic." More strikingly, he (Gorbachev) held a private meeting in Canada earlier in the week with one of the leading gurus of the New Age Movement, Sri Chinmoy, who read him a "spiritual song" and gave him a volume of admiring letters.[12]

During President Gorbachev's recent visit to the United States, in Los Angeles, he told an international TV audience that mankind was indeed entering a New Age and that man's "mind" would have to change accordingly. Then, just before the historic Malta summit conference with George Bush, Gorbachev went to the Vatican and met with Pope John Paul II. At that earth-shaking conclave, Gorbachev not only shared his vision of Europe as a "united commonwealth," but he also laid claim to certain world "spiritual values." "What we need," declared Gorbachev, "is a revolution of the mind." He added: "This is the only way toward a new culture and new politics that can meet the challenge of our time."[13]

When President George Bush and Mikhail Gorbachev

met at Malta the headline in the *New York Times* trumpeted "Superpowers Forge New World Order." Yes, just as I revealed, Soviet leader Mikhail Gorbachev has unquestionably become the world's foremost New Age political leader pushing for a World Order.

The implications of this are mind-boggling. To acquire Western capital (money!) he is pretending to be a champion of religious freedom. But this is all a subterfuge for Gorbachev's real intent. He and co-conspirators want to establish a One World Order under which there will eventually be only *one* religion allowed--a New Age religion that excludes Jesus Christ, Lord of lords and King of kings.

Gorbachev Meets With Cultists

Gorbachev continues to promote the Marxist deception that man can solve his own problems without divine assistance. In New York, he declared, "The United Nations should set up a Global Brain Trust of scientists, politicians, and even church leaders to help solve global problems." In 1988 he sent Soviet delegates to a global New Age convocation called "The Global Spiritual and Parliamentary Forum on Human Survival," which met in Oxford, England.

The Soviet President is quick to grant private audiences to New Age religious and political bigwigs. Recently he met privately in Moscow with the Reverend Sun Myung Moon of the Unification Church (CAUSA). After the meeting, the leader of the Moonies, a New Age cult, noted that Gorbachev had stressed the need for a "New World Order."

First, Satan used dictators Vladimir Lenin and Joseph Stalin to drive freedom of religion from Russia, creating a shell of atheism and agnosticism. Today, that shell is now finally being filled with unadulterated New Age lies and occultic/globalist doctrine. A new "State religion" is being formed. Who is head of this emerging, New Age Soviet State religion, its Archbishop so to speak?--President Mikhail Gorbachev, named by *Time* magazine as its 1987 "Man of the Year."

What Does the Word "Perestroika" Really Stand For?

In a stunning book that has become a bestseller in the United States, Gorbachev frankly sets forth his New Age worldview. Published in America by Harper & Row, a major U.S. publisher, the book is titled, *Perestroika: New Thinking For Our Country and the World.* An examination of this book, combined with Gorbachev's acts and deeds since assuming his high position in Moscow, leads us to the inevitable conclusion that Satan's demonic powers have found their mark in the charismatic and fertile, but evil mind of Comrade Gorbachev.

Enthusiastically endorsing the world peace movement, in his book Gorbachev announces that the issue of disarmament and world peace "can and must rally mankind, and facilitate the formation of a *global consciousness."*

He further makes clear that his concept of global consciousness is the same as that of such fervent New Age theologians and teachers as Benjamin Creme, David Spangler, and Barbara Marx Hubbard, when he calls for acceptance of a new worldview:

> In the nuclear age, humanity must evolve a new mode of political thought, a new concept of the world ... a new way of thinking.[14]

In *Perestroika*, Gorbachev uses almost every buzzword and catch-phrase made popular by New Age thinkers, even to the extent of abusing biblical terminology:

This world is . . . one whole. We are all passengers aboard
one ship, the Earth, and we must not allow it to be
wrecked. There will be no second Noah's Ark.[15]

The Soviet leader speaks of "God" (though not the
God of the Bible) and emphasizes the "restructuring of
moral values." His god is that of human potential. Like
other New Agers, he believes that man is a sleeping god
unaware of his divinity:

People, human beings with all their creative diversity, are
the maker of history. So the initial task of restructuring . . .
is to "wake up" those people who have "fallen asleep" and
make them truly active and concerned, to ensure that
everyone feels as if he is the master of the country, of his
enterprise, office, or institute. This is the main thing.[16]

What, then, does *Perestroika* mean? Secretary
Gorbachev explains:

Perestroika is a *revolution*. A decisive acceleration of the
socio-economic and cultural development of Soviet society
which involves radical changes *on the way to a qualitatively
new state*.[17]

He goes on to say that this is not only a Soviet, but a
world-wide revolution equally as far-reaching as former
great social, political, and religious upheavals in France
(the Great Revolution of 1789-93), Great Britain (Crom-
well's Revolution of 1649 and the "Glorious Revolution"
of 1688-89) and Germany (Bismark's "iron and blood"
reform of the late 1860s).

The shrewd Soviet overlord declares that "the whole
world needs restructuring" and he points the way to a *new
reality*, explaining that:

We know that we in this world are, on the whole, now
linked to the same destiny, that we live on the same

planet ... that such a reality holds for all of us ... For the whole world needs restructuring.[18]

A New Way of Thinking

According to the Soviet Communist chieftain, the "New Way of Thinking" will promote new universal values to take advantage of man's "spiritual capital," a kind of resource built up, he says, without the need for a personal God: "Amazing things happen, when people take responsibility for everything themselves," he contends. What is needed, Gorbachev stresses, is the kind of revolution that *alters men's minds:*

A new way of thinking must develop ... Revolutions always begin *in the mind ... in liberating the mind.*[19]

Soviet leader Mikhail Gorbachev has volunteered to lead the whole world into this revolution to liberate man's mind. At the massive 27th Congress of the Communist Party of the Soviet Union, he had his nation's entire governmental apparatus boldly announce that the Soviet Union officially endorses the:

--establishment of a new world economic order guaranteeing economic security to all countries; and the

--extirpation (ending) of genocide, apartheid, advocacy of fascism and every other form of racial, *national or religious exclusiveness,* and also of discrimination against people on this basis.[20]

American New Agers and Globalists Back Gorbachev

Gorbachev is putting wings on his New Age ideas. For one thing, he eagerly addresses Western peace delegations that visit Moscow. He sent 300 Soviet citizen delegates to a mammothly publicized New Age event held in Washington, D.C. on February 1-5, 1988. California State legislator John Vasconcellos, former U.N. diplomat Dr. Robert Muller, broadcaster Ted Turner, scientist Willis Harman, pop psychologist Gerald Jampolsky, author Gail Sheehy, and other American New Age activists hosted this event which took as its theme the work necessary to *converge* Soviet and U.S. interests and to "shift Soviet-American consciousness from separation and fear to unity and love." One of the workshops was revealingly entitled, "Religion, Atheism, and Spirituality."

In 1987, Soviet Leader Gorbachev met with a large group of U.S. celebrities in Moscow. He outlined to them his new worldview and asked them to help him propagate the new Soviet "gospel." "You are well-known in your own country, and your voice is needed," he urged. Among the well-known celebrities who attended were economist John Kenneth Galbraith, scientist Carl Sagan, actor Paul Newman, singer John Denver, two former U.S. Secretaries of State, Henry Kissinger and Cyrus Vance, and former Secretary of Defense Robert McNamara. Regrettably, also at the gala was evangelist Billy Graham, who once upon a time bravely condemned globalism, communism, and ecumenicism, but has recently softened his views considerably.

Reportedly, the reception was not marked by dissent. Not one of these American visitors, for example, complained to Gorbachev of the continuing Soviet persecution of Jews and fundamentalist Christians as well as the Soviet's continued occupation of such captive nations as the Baltic Republics. Yet, all were obliged to listen to the Soviet Party Chief encourage all present to be "united in our thoughts and actions."

Gorbachev's repeated call for a "Global Brain Trust" of "Nobel laureates, diplomats and churchmen" to help focus the world's attention on peace, disarmament, and similar issues is especially revealing. This is startingly similar to the proposals of the Lucis Trust and other New Age groups for a "World Mind" or "Council of Wise Persons" to oversee the peace process and set up a One World economic and political order.

Gorbachev's New Age Emissary to America

Gorbachev has also begun to send special citizen "evangelists" steeped in New Age and occult religious doctrines to America where they meet with kindred spirits. One premier example is the U.S. visit of famed Soviet poet, Igor Mikhailusenko. *New Frontier* magazine reported on Mikhailusenko's visit to various New Age communes amd communities and interviewed him regarding his upcoming Soviet book, *The Best of American Freedom*. In the interview, Mikhailusenko parroted the official Soviet party line, but with a remarkable difference from that of just a few years ago, announcing that anything "New Age" is "in" in the U.S.S.R.[21]

Keep in mind that Mikhailusenko, the bestselling author in Russia today, was sent as an *official* Soviet representative. Therefore, we can possibly glean from his comments the type of propaganda now being pushed inside the Soviet Union to its own people. Here are just a few of the Russian poet's statements to the interviewer:

I trust in Supermind.

The Force is God. But it's a Cosmic God.

I hold great respect for all religions and I even have a little bronze Buddha from the Peace Pagoda.

I'm quite certain that the earth now goes not into an abyss, but moves to a brighter future. . . . I have a glorious vision that by the year 2000 the world will surely reach its destination. It will be a world without weapons where all dwellers on earth, all peoples and nations, will be happy and free and will live in prosperity.

Mikhailusenko, however, didn't just stop at reciting these common New Age themes. He went on to discuss astral travel (he claimed out-of-body experiences), the Peace Movement, spaceship earth, and higher consciousness.

As the views of Mikhailusenko indicate, even if Gorbachev falls, his successor will no doubt echo the new party line from the Kremlin. Indeed, when Gorbachev's principal political opponent Boris Yeltsin recently came to America, the trip was sponsored and paid for by a California-based New Age organization.

Planetary Transformation and The Occult Theocracy

How can our world leaders be so blatantly unholy? Has the whole world gone insane? No, the world is not insane, at least from a Biblical perspective. It has simply entered the slimy era when Satan is given practically free reign. This is why everywhere we turn, we find prominent people in all fields endorsing the goals of the conspirators and immersing themselves in various New Age and occultic philosophies and religious practices. The awful truth is that an incredible planetary transformation has *already* taken place while so many of us were unaware.

PART TWO

The Money Crash and the New World Order

SEVEN

When Will the Dollar Die?

And that no man might buy or sell, save he that had the mark, or the name of the beast, or the number of his name.

(Revelation 13:17)

Today we have paper money that essentially has no value to it . . . a source (at the Federal Reserve) friendly to us stated confidentially there is going to be a new paper currency. It is going to be a different color . . . It has been studied for six years.

Congressman Ron Paul
The Coming Currency Exchange

The day the dollar died no one came to its funeral. Indeed, the sad but inescapable fact is that few realized that the dollar had passed away. Even today many who cherish the dollar the most are blissfully unaware of its demise. Those who are the most gullible and unquestioning are convinced that the dollar will live forever, that it is like an eternal living creature whose vibrancy and energetic bounce will be seen, felt, and heard throughout the world for eons to come. But they are wrong. The dollar is dead. We have only to await its funeral. Even now, if we listen closely enough we can hear the first stanzas of the inevitable dirge and burial music.

No one but its assassins are quite sure of the exact

moment and date the dollar died. Those in the know have come to the conclusion that the life-force of the dollar first began to ebb away slowly and inexorably sometime in January 1980. During that eventful month an amazing event occurred in the world's marketplaces. Men everywhere began to clamor for gold, the most precious metal. The world's speculators and investors, as well as the little man and woman on the street, bid up the price of gold to an astounding high of $875 an ounce. It seemed as if the word was out. The dollar was in very desperate shape. For their own economic and financial salvation, the world had turned to the only commodity which throughout the centuries has assured safety and preservation. Gold.

Massive government debt and conspiratorial acts by a small clan of international schemers had succeeded in destroying much of the value of the U.S. dollar. Thus, many people began to turn to gold as a hedge against economic and financial disaster. They also began to turn to other currencies and particularly to the German mark and the Japanese yen.

Those who plotted its death saw to it that a second blow was dealt the dollar in August, 1982. Just as the International Monetary Fund (IMF) was about to convene its annual meeting in Toronto, Canada, that month, Mexico, a third world nation that owed $64 billion to the United States and other central banks, shocked the financial community. Mexico declared itself unable to meet its massive debt obligations. Brazil and a host of other major borrower nations quickly followed suit.

Michael Claudon, editor of an extensive study of the world debt crisis, subsequently wrote, "Those declarations pushed the world banking system to the brink of financial chaos . . . the global debt crisis was grave."[1]

Claudon noted that the nine largest U.S. money center banks had lent some $98.6 billion of their bank capital to third world nations in the preceding decade--more than these banks had assets! Now it was time to pay the piper. Those nations were unable to pay their just debts.

"Therefore," said Claudon, "on paper, at least, these nine banks were bankrupt after the fateful declarations of August, 1982."

In the years since 1982 it has become even more apparent to insiders that the dollar is dead and that we are living on borrowed time. They will come soon to take our money away. They will drag off the carcass. And in its wake, issue us a worthless bunch of newer paper certificates. In fact, that is practically all the greenback is today-- a worthless piece of paper with esoteric symbols printed thereon in green ink. But the "New Money," when it is issued, will be worth even less.

In his book, *Delicate Balance: Coming Catastrophic Changes on Planet Earth*, John Zajac warns:

> The financial system of the free world is on the verge of a major catastrophe. In fact, it almost collapsed in the summer of 1983 and the U.S. Government Printing Office (GPO) was ready to print 'new' money in case it did.[2]

Zajac explained that the U.S. dollar is not backed by gold or silver, but only by the faith of the people that it is stable and it is acceptable in trade. If the major banks suffer catastrophic losses and are forced to close their doors, then people would quickly lose faith in the dollar and thousands of other banks would be forced to close their doors as people begin to storm the doors seeking assurances that their deposits would be made good. "All it would take," says Zajac, "to collapse the world's financial system is the realization that paper money is only paper:"

> After all, that is all it is. It has no intrinsic value, unlike something that can be used, manufactured, or eaten. Most wealth is not even in the form of money anymore; it is represented by a piece of paper (deposit slip) that a bank gives you symbolizing the wealth that you gave to it. Since the bank lent your money to somebody else, it cannot

return it to you anymore. The person who borrowed your money from your bank bought something, and the person or company who sold it to him put the money in some other bank and received another paper deposit slip. That bank immediately lent the money to someone else. Today in America, every paper dollar is claimed by at least six sources: the person who deposited it, the bank, the person who sold something to the borrower from the bank, this third person's bank, the person who borrowed from the second bank, and the person who sold goods or services to the second bank's borrower.[3]

Congressman Ron Paul once asked the Assistant Secretary of the Treasury, Barry Sprinkle, if a Federal Reserve Note, which is what our dollars are called nowadays, are redeemable in anything tangible such as gold or silver. Paul reported Sprinkle's response as follows: "He chuckled and laughed and said, 'Yes, it is convertible into another federal reserve note.' That is his answer to a very serious question." But, Paul reflected, "someday, enough people will wake up and realize this is not a laughing matter."[4]

The New Money is On Its Way

Get ready in the near future for what is being called the New Money to be issued. You see, the dollar has slid in value so sharply that it is on its last legs. Therefore the world's largest corporations and most influential investment and financial community officials have lost faith in the dollar. I believe this has been the plot all along of the elite group of men who control the world's future. They have brought the dollar to the very point of total collapse. Their ultimate purpose is to create a one world currency, a New Money, which will be issued to all the people of the world. This money will be sharply controlled by the few megabanks that are left after the current shake-out of banks is completed and thousands of small banks around the United States and even the world have gone bankrupt and are out of business. This New Money will be issued only to those who are willing to kow-tow to those who control it.

Only by the grace of God has this new money not been issued up to now. Evidently, God has His own time-table as to when these last days events will occur. Thus, there has been a delay in the plans of the schemers. Again and again they have been forced to delay the implementation of the New Money.

Congressman Ron Paul, formerly a U.S. representative from the state of Texas, became intimately involved with the new money. A member of the prestigious and powerful banking committee of the U.S. House of Representatives, Congressman Paul was able to conduct and chair congressional hearings on the New Money. Here is his testimony:

> Today we have paper money that essentially has no value to it.... Over the years I have been extremely interested in monetary policy. I am on the Domestic Monetary Policy Subcommittee dealing with these issues. Unfortunately, I sometimes feel that the people and even the congress is left on the outside. As you know, the Federal Reserve System is a very powerful system and *they* control the money.

> Over the years I have had many constituents write and ask me to find out what is happening with the money and the possibility of a new currency. At the beginning I thought this was way up in the future and we were not ready for a new currency. But then in congress we heard rumors that this money was already printed and stored in the vault. But anytime somebody from the Treasury or the Federal Reserve would appear before the banking committee I would inquire about it, and it was always denied.

I have been doing this for three or four years and never got
any information until about Thanksgiving of 1983. My
office placed a call to the Federal Reserve. A source
friendly to us stated confidentially, 'you know, its true.
There is going to be a new paper currency. It is going to be
a different color... It has been studied for the past six
years, and a committee has been set up.[5]

Congressman Ron Paul believes that certain forces
have intentionally destroyed our money: "This is what is
happening, I believe a change in color is definitely an
attack on our personal freedoms."[6]

The Coming Great Money Swap

What is going to take place, apparently, is that the federal
government of the United States will recall all of the
money currently in use. Suddenly on a given day the
government will announce over the national television
networks that all the money previously in circulation, the
greenbacks, are totally worthless and can no longer be
used to buy goods or services. Everyone will be required
to go to their nearest bank or savings and loan or other
special office set up by the government in their local area
and exchange their green dollars for the new dollars which
will be of a totally new color.

Some have reported that the color will be blue or pink.
The New Money will also have metal strips in it so that its
value and other important information can be read by the
automatic teller machines (ATM) at banks and at the
supermarket, department stores and elsewhere.

Frighteningly, there is also going to be a small space
left blank on the dollar. In fact, this is already the case in
the currency of many other countries. Newer currency
overseas in these countries has been issued in which a
small blank space, a white area, has been left vacant on

the currency notes. Nobody is fully revealing what this blank area is to be used for. But every nation that is issuing currency today is leaving in this blank space.

Could it be that this space will someday be used for a special numbering system that will be used to bring together all of the world's currencies into one? Might there be a picture of a certain individual placed in that empty space on all world currency to denote an allegiance to *one* world leader? The answer to these momentous questions, I believe, can be found in the Bible--in the book of Revelation, chapter 13.

Money is Control . . . and Power

It goes without saying that *whoever controls the money controls the country.* Congressman Ron Paul himself noted this fact when he said, "if you control the money, you actually control every transaction that exists in this country."[7] That is why this is such an important issue. If you control the money, you can do practically anything you want with the people.

Yes, there is power in money. The power of money can be very oppressive. A few years ago, the influential *Washington Post* newspaper printed an article entitled *The Coloring of Greenbacks,* which discussed the possibility of the New Money being issued and the old recalled. Interestingly enough, the article began with a very cryptic phrase, "Oh money, we love you, we hate you, and we are ever conscious of your power."[8]

For hundreds of years, kings, emperors, popes, military dictators, and assorted madmen have established control over the most minute details of everyday human lives by controlling the issue and use of money. *Money is control.*

Satan certainly understands this key principle. It was in 1748 that Emmanuel Swedenbourg, a Swedish mystic today revered by many in New Age and Illuminati circles wrote:

> I spoke with spirits concerning the possession of money.... Certain spirits are of such a character derived from the light of the body (when their spirits were in human flesh) that they wish to possess money, for money's sake, not for any other use, than to be delighted with money.... They have said that they have desired it on account of delight at the sight of money, silver, and gold.[9]

When Will the New Money be Issued?

As Congressman Paul noted, it is extremely difficult to get to the truth about when and how the New Money will be issued. In mid-1987 I began to communicate with the Department of the Treasury in Washington, D.C., to see if I could get to the bottom of the New Money situation. After encountering some delays and rather cloudy answers on the part of treasury officials, finally, on June 16, 1987 I received a letter from the Department of the Treasury, Bureau of Engraving and Printing in Washington, D.C., confirming that there were indeed plans afoot to create a new money. Here below is a portion of this letter.

> Last March, the Department of the Treasury announced changes would be made to United States paper currency. First, a clear polyester thread would be incorporated into the paper, arranged vertically through a narrow clear field on the notes, and could be seen by the human eye when the note is held to a light source. The thread would contain printed information consisting of the letters 'U.S.A.,' and the denominational value of that specific note. Second, the words 'United States of America' would be microprinted repeatedly (in a circle) around the portrait on the face of the note.

The purpose of these changes is to continue to protect the public's currency transactions by deterring counterfeiting. The development of advanced color copying machines that permit high resolution color reproduction, even by unskilled operators, is rapidly increasing. The future of widespread availability of such copiers threatens to create a new kind of problem involving so-called 'casual' counterfeiters. These features will deter this problem.

Concurrently, the Bureau is in the process of procuring production quantities of the threaded paper. Additional time will be required by potential suppliers of the paper to complete development and pass the stringent quality requirements of the Bureau of Engraving and Printing. At that time, a press release will be issued announcing the Bureau's production schedule.

This letter was followed up by other information supplied to me in which Katherine D. Ortega, Treasurer of the United States, revealed that production of the New Money had been impeded by the inability to assure superior quality bank notes which could include security threads at high speed production levels. Up to an additional two years, she claimed, would be required to complete this process. Then Ortega made an interesting final comment. "The Bureau will continue to print the 1985 series of Federal Reserve Notes *until further notice.*"

Why the delay in issuing the New Money? I think the manipulators realize that the American people will be extremely upset when they find out that the New Money has very little value and in fact can not purchase as many goods and services as did the old money. In other words, when this money is issued, it may very well be that the dollar is severely devalued. Thus for every $10 in greenbacks you have now, you might be issued $100 of the new funny money, so-called, of a different color. At first you exclaim, "Wonderful! Now I have ten times as much money as I had before." But of course, what you might not realize is that everything will go up in price. Not just by a value of ten, but by as much as 20 or 30 times.

A Financial Crisis is Needed

You would therefore find that your dollars cannot be stretched to cover even the barest of necessities for living. For this reason it is necessary to soften up the American people and prepare them for the blow so that there will be no widespread rebellion. To do this, it will be necessary to cause a *monetary crisis* of some sort. Then people will be willing to undergo any kind of change just to get some financial relief. As we will shortly see, another Great Depression could very well be the kind of crisis that is needed to bully the American people into accepting the New Money.

Facing financial crisis and disaster, the average American may well decide that the New Money is better than no money at all. And this is exactly what the manipulators hope to implant in the minds of the disheartened and frightened everyday American.

Given these facts, we can begin to understand why the Department of the Treasury has been silent on this issue. As the stock market boomed to the 3000 mark in the Dow Jones averages, and prosperity seemed to be guaranteed to all Americans in the 1980s, it was impossible for the New Money to be issued. As Katherine Ortega, Treasury of the United States, stated, the old series of money would continue to be printed "until further notice."

However, as soon as the current economic boom is brought to a screeching halt, then the government and the megabanks will move swiftly to issue the New Money and defraud the American public. Bill Baxter, in his *Baxter Economic* newsletter, explains this as follows:

Government spokesmen will insist until the very last
moment that no recall is planned. But this is the practice
of all governments. They can not announce in advance that
a currency is going to be recalled or devalued. It would
create havoc in the financial markets. Such announcements
are usually without warning and when the financial
markets are closed.[10]

Baxter continues:

The Roosevelt administration made everyone turn in their
gold in the 1930s. After the people had done so, the
government jacked up the price, pulling off one of the
most bald-faced robberies of its citizenry since the colonies
were settled. Then in the 1960s, the government said that
all the silver certificates that were convertible into silver
bullion had to be turned in.[11]

Justifying The Need for New Money

The controllers, the men manipulating our money supply,
will not only be aided by the coming world financial crisis
and money panic, but they will also be able to successfully
claim a number of other benefits for the New Money. For
example, as we have seen, the Treasury Department is
already mentioning the possibility of counterfeiting on
new color copiers.

Another excuse will be that the New Money will cut
out money laundering, the use by drug smugglers,
embezzlers, and defrauders of greenbacks. When the new
money is issued and the old declared worthless, then
everyone will be required to go and register their old
money and exchange it for the new. Then the IRS will be
able to find out who has the money that has been hidden
and squirreled away. The criminals can be uncovered, it is
claimed.

The fact is, the truth is far different. The international criminals have most of their money deposited safely in the megabanks. Only a small percent of their income is kept in actual dollar bills, that is greenbacks. Just as has been the case in the past, the drug dealers will be able to keep their ill-gotten gains, because they are colluding *electronically* with the bankers. Many will be protected from the coming currency exchange because they will receive advance word of the date.

The honest working men and women will suffer the most as the great currency robbery takes place. As one expert, Ingo Walter revealed in his book, *The Secret Money Market*, there is a dark world of tax evasion, financial fraud, insider stock market trading, money laundering, and capital flight that exists. Walter reveals that this dark side of high finance includes government officials and financial institutions on an international level who are only too happy to handle secret financial transactions. These transactions usually take place electronically as a blizzard of computer entries are made. A smart criminal has no need of the actual bank notes or greenbacks.[12]

No Cash Needed

Ultimately of course, all paper money will be done away with and people will receive a mark just as is foretold in Revelation 13. Smart cards, as they are dubbed, have already been developed by Hitachi, Texas Instruments, and other computer corporations. The plan is to eliminate cash altogether in favor of computerized, so-called theft-proof "smart cards." These cards appear much like your Visa, Mastercard or Discover credit cards. They contain holographic images, bar codes, and/or metal strips as well as microchips which are inserted therein which can be read and contain a marvelous amount of information on the individual.

William Raspberry, editorialist for the *Washington Post* newspaper, recently wrote about the plans for this smart card. As he explained it, the claims are that it "would bust up organized crime, put an end to the deadly traffic in illegal drugs, reduce espionage and terrorism, drastically curtail corruption and tax evasion, and begin a return to civility." According to the people pushing the smart cards:

> Cash is the root of a heck of a lot of the world's evil . . . They would outlaw it in phases: large bills first, then successively smaller ones and, finally, coins. In it's place: smart cards . . . On a folded card, the size of a dollar bill would be imprinted an astonishing amount of information: your bank balances, credit limits, medical records, passport, driver's license, photographs, welfare eligibility, and other data including--this is key--your thumbprint. The thumbprint would have to be verified electronically with each transaction and this supposedly would make the card worthless to a thief.[13]

Ominously, Raspberry reported that "every single transaction would create its own record which could then be used for criminal investigations, just as checks, bank accounts, and credit card records are used now."[14]

The money manipulators would have us believe that the smart cards have inestimable benefits:

> The benefits of replacing cash would be incalculable. No cash to smuggle. The sale of illegal drugs would stop since no one would want a record of its transaction. The spread of AIDS would be curtailed as drug abuse ends. The cost of government would go down, as would the cost of private business. Tax evasion, payment in cash to avoid sales tax, or failure to report cash income would cease. The national debt could be reduced: stolen items could not be sold

without a trace. Personal security would be assured. Little old ladies could walk in the park again.[15]

This is what the powerful money men envision for us. It seems like a Utopia come true. First issue the New Money, then take away *all* the money. The aims seem to be good ones. Certainly the rising lawlessness in our society is a threat to our liberty. How many realize that the control of money, which would be nearly complete with such an electronic smart card system, is exactly what the Bible prophesied would occur in the last days?

Yes, the build-up is definitely in progress to convince the American people of the need for the New Money. The signal that The Order is about ready to give the go-ahead came, I believe, when Donald Regan, former White House chief of staff, stock brokerage executive and insider with CFR, went public with a proposal for a currency exchange. Here is a news account of Regan's proposal:

WASHINGTON (AP)--Donald T. Regan, who served as treasury secretary and White House chief of staff in the Reagan administration, proposed Monday that the government change the color or size of $50 and $100 bills to frustrate drug dealers with big accumulations of currency.

Under Regan's proposal, the government would announce that the old bills would be worthless in 10 days.

When people went to banks to exchange their bills for the new currency, records would be made of all transactions involving more than $1,000--forcing drug dealers to either give up vast fortunes or expose themselves to scrutiny by law enforcement agencies.

This would panic those with huge cash holdings, Regan said.

"No one should have any fear. Yes, it might cause confusion for a couple of months, but what honest citizen wouldn't be willing to put up with a little inconvenience so as to trap these criminals?" Regan wrote.

"This would hit the criminals where it hurts most--in the pocketbook."

Additionally, Regan proposed an agreement of all central banks in industrialized nations to instruct member banks not to accept deposits "from known, or suspected drug dealers and not to do business with any banks . . . that accept drug money."[16]

The Plot To Destroy America As A Nation

If an international group of schemers, which includes unpatriotic Americans filled with greed for money and possessed by a lust for power, decide to destroy America, what is the best way they could proceed? The answer: suck the very life-blood out of the U.S. dollar.

This is in fact exactly what is now occurring. There has been an ongoing assault against the dollar for more than a decade. It is apparent that the controllers have decided it is now time to merge the United States economy with the New International Economic Order. All are to be one. To do this, the almighty dollar must be destroyed in value. It must be taken down a few notches, whittled down to size, so that as compared with the rising German mark and the sky-high Japanese yen it will look like a pygmy in comparison. Then Americans will gladly merge to get the benefits of the more affluent mark and yen. Next, the plotters will suggest: "Wouldn't it be better yet to have just *one currency* for everyone?"

The dollar has been in an unparalleled freefall and has

now hit record lows against many of the world's currencies. Why would the leaders of any government collaborate in the destruction of their own currency? Perhaps this is a question we should ask our own president and leaders. In 1989 officials at the Federal Reserve Board and at the Department of the Treasury consistently took actions in concert with the finance ministers of the Group of Seven countries to bring down the value of the dollar. In fact, at the end of September, 1989 Treasury Secretary Nicholas Brady, a member of the CFR and the Trilateral Commission, issued a statement reaffirming our government's determination to bring down the value of the dollar and resist any temporary rise in its value.[17]

This brings us back to the question of the New Money. You will recall that Congressman Ron Paul revealed that his congressional committee had verified rumors that plans have been made for a new currency to be issued. This currency would not be green, but would instead be blue, or perhaps pink. It would be manufactured in such a way that it could be controlled electronically. Paul has said, "the new currency is definitely in our future."[18]

At the time Paul conducted his hearings, the foundation had not yet been laid by The Order in terms of propaganda, the setting up of various international institutions, and so forth. Today, I am convinced that the world has now been set up, preparations have been made. All that is necessary is that the small cartel of wicked financial rulers in the top echelons give the "go" signal. When they do, the crisis will occur fast and furiously.

Congressman Ron Paul, in his hearings, questioned the Federal Reserve treasury officials and Secret Service officials who testified. "When," he insisted, "will the new paper currency be issued?" The Federal Reserve answered that question by saying it would be gradual. But, Paul notes that someone sitting next to him in the Secret Service, who has a lot more to do with it, leaned over to him and quietly whispered in his ear, "No, it has to be very rapid."[19]

EIGHT

Signs of Impending Disaster

So likewise ye, when ye shall see all these things: know that it is near, even at the doors.

(Matthew 24:33)

What is happening to the U.S.A.'s banks? Once they stood like the Colossus, straddling the oceans to dominate the world's financial marketplaces. In 1956 five of the top ten banks in the world were U.S. banks. In 1978 there were three; today, none are.

U.S.A. Today
May 29, 1990

In the Gospels of Matthew and Luke, Jesus told us the signs of His second coming. He described these signs as similar to birth pains that occur during labor of a pregnant woman. When the contractions occur, then you begin to realize that a major event is soon to take place. Christ cited a number of such contractions that would occur in the last days. Then He concluded "So likewise ye, when ye shall see all these things: know that it is near, even at the doors" (Matthew 24:33).

It is manifestly evident that the signs Jesus gave us of the impending last days before His second coming are the same ones we are seeing today. One of the greatest signs of all in Bible prophecy is an approaching *economic Armageddon* that occurs following what appears to be an unparalleled era of peace and prosperity.

Certainly this is the situation today. As I write this book, we see the stock market at all-time high levels. Men and women throughout the United States, Western Europe, and in many other nations of the world believe that the good times will never end, that things are going to get better and better. But that is not what the Bible tells us. The Bible says that after a short space in which things seem to be lovely and beautiful, then great tribulations will begin, leading up to Jesus' return.

There can be nothing more clear than the fact that a great *Global Depression* is on the way. We have been standing on the edge of a cliff. The view looks terrific. But there is a cruel and selfish group of men led by supernatural forces who are going to push us off the cliff, and the fall will end with a thud and with pain and sorrow if we are not prepared.

Let us take a look to see if we can detect the signs of this coming Global Depression and the tremendous economic slump that lies just ahead. What we must do is look at a number of indicators that show us the days are truly very, very short.

The Great Savings & Loan Scam

Americans have their money stored primarily in two types of institutions: Savings & Loans and Banks. If we really wish to see the dastardly state of the American economy, we need only go to these two sectors of the economy. When we do, we come away with a most shocking discovery. *Both the savings & loan institutions and our banks have already failed.* They are living on borrowed time. They are like a dead body that is rotting because the funeral has been put off far, far too long by the undertaker.

On December 22, 1989 a headline in newspapers across the country trumpeted "Savings & Loans (S&L) losses pile up despite bailout." The Associated Press reported that despite massive federal bailouts approved by President Bush and Congress, the savings & loan industry has lost $3.8 billion in the July through September 1989 quarter. All in all, the 1989 S&L losses were the greatest in all of United States history. Ominously, the report stated, "Industry analysts said they saw little prospect for return to profitability any time soon." One analyst, Burt Ely from Alexandria, Virginia, commented, "it is like a water torture. It is going to continue quarter after quarter after quarter."[1]

Ely's prediction certainly was borne out. On March 27, 1990 USA Today carried the headline "Lenders Tighten the Purse Strings," followed by another story, "S&Ls Still Suffer, Despite Bailout." In the latter story, the newspaper reported: "Despite the government's $160 billion bailout, the savings & loan industry continues to hemorrhage. The U.S.A.'s 2,878 S&Ls lost a record $19.2 billion last year, according to data released by the Office of Thrift Supervision." Moreover, USA Today stated that "even the roughly 2,400 'healthy' S&Ls aren't that healthy."[2]

Burt Ely, who several months before had used the term "water torture" to describe the continuing S&L crisis, was quoted by U.S.A. Today as reacting: "There is disturbing news here. The cancer is spreading."

According to the same report, 281 S&Ls were seized by the government because of financial red ink. Another 120 S&Ls were targeted for seizure during the coming year.

All in all, many financial experts believe that the collapse of the savings & loan industry could cost American taxpayers up to one trillion dollars (that is ten hundred billion). Nathaniel Nash of the New York Times compiled a story for international release that the Resolution Trust Corporation, established by Congress to manage the savings & loan bailout, will have to take over almost 1,000 institutions before the end will be in sight. What Nash failed to do was to describe exactly *what end* will result from this S&L catastrophe.

The Bumpy Road For Banks

Savings & loan institutions are joined in their misery by our banks. As I have traveled the United States the past three years, I heard tale after tale of people discovering that their neighborhood bank has gone out of business and has closed down its doors. Many hundreds of banks are no longer in operation.

Significantly, during the Great Depression of the 1930s, most banks were quite healthy until the depression was well under way. Not so today. We are only on the outer edge of the Great Depression, and already our banks are collapsing at an alarming rate. Over $250 billion has already been lost by the banks, a scandal that is caused by mismanagement and fraud as well as by design.

In its cover story for its money section on May 29, 1990, *USA Today* broadcast the news that:

> Bad loans, competition take their toll on the nation's banks. Every day the news seems to get worse about the financial condition of the U.S.A.'s banks. Bad real estate loans are skyrocketing, earnings are falling, banks are failing. And the Federal Fund that insures bank deposits covers only 70 cents of every $100 it insures--the lowest level of protection since the Great Depression.[3]

We cannot trust the government to tell us the truth about the impending financial calamity. Only a year before, lawmakers, banking experts, and government regulatory officials had denied that there was a major problem with U.S. banks. The experts answered an emphatic "no." Only a few are brave enough to admit the churning chaos and boiling cauldron in which we find ourselves.

Statistics show the extent of the impending crisis. In the five years from 1985 to 1990, 791 banks failed; 540 more are reported by regulatory agencies to have problem loans and reserve problems. What that means is that they simply don't have the money to meet their obligations.

Here is the sad state of affairs, as commented on by *USA Today:*

> What is happening to the U.S.A.'s banks? Once they stood like the Colossus, straddling the oceans to dominate the world's financial marketplaces. In 1956, five of the top ten banks in the world were U.S. banks; in 1978, three were; today, none are.

"A nation with a second rate banking system is a second rate nation," says Comptroller of the Currency Robert Clark. Economist Dan Brumbaugh agrees: "We are in the midst of a very important emergency," he warns.[4]

The full extent of the banking crisis is little understood by the public. The fact is that the Federal Deposit Insurance Corporation (FDIC) backs the trillions of dollars of bank deposits with only about $13.2 billion now in its insurance fund. In event of a depression, there is no way that this will be enough to cover all the losses. The same holds true for the Federal Savings & Loan Insurance Corporation (FSLIC), which was created to assure depositors that even though their savings & loan might go bankrupt, all of their money would not be lost.

When the savings & loan debacle recently mushroomed out of control, the FSLIC actually became insolvent and Congress had to rush billions of new dollars to its aid to clean up the S&L mess, which has already passed the $500 billion mark (together the banks and S&Ls are in the red $750 billion and that stupendous amount is growing!). Sometime in the near future, expect a big run on the banks and savings & loans that are left, as the crisis hits with all of its mighty impact. You may well find that there is not only no money at the cashier's window, but that the promise of the politicians to repay you from the insurance funds backed by government agencies FDIC and FSLIC will suddenly come up null and void.

The New Money is Issued: Take It or Nothing!

Now how would they handle such an emergency--one that is sure to occur sometime this decade? The answer, of course, is: they will issue the *New Money*. You won't be able to get greenbacks from your failed bank or savings & loan, but they will be willing to issue you the new pink or blue money and you will have to take it because it is all they will have available to you. Take it or leave it.

Oh yes, there are evidently eleven banks, the eleven largest in this country, that will *not* fail. Meanwhile, hundreds of small banks throughout America are forced to close their doors; they are being gobbled up and merged with these few remaining giants. Comptroller of the Currency Todd Conover has told the House Banking Committee of Congress that these eleven banks are considered "too big to fail by the government."

This was an amazing statement since, as I have noted, the eleven largest banks in America are owed billions by third-world nations which are unable to pay them back. In fact, nine of these eleven large banks have lent out *220 percent* of their total combined equity to third-world nations and to the bankrupt nations of Russia and Eastern Europe.

If you are wondering who the "illustrious" eleven megabanks are, here is the list:

* Bank of America   * First National of Chicago
* Banker's Trust   * Manufacturer's Hanover Trust
* Chase Manhattan   * Morgan Guaranty
* Citibank   * Security Pacific
* Chemical Bank   * Wells Fargo
* Continental

It should come as no surprise to you and I that the Federal Reserve Bank was created primarily to prevent these huge institutions from failing. Moreover, the owners of these eleven banks, as well as foreign interests, also own all the shares of the Federal Reserve Bank, and its directors are chosen by them.

What we can look for, then, at some future moment in time, is for these megabanks, owned by The Order, to oversee the distribution of the New Money to U.S. citizens. This will be accomplished through their thousands of branch banks, which once were friendly neighborhood banks before they were forced out of business.

The Megabank Takeover

The Lords of Money who run the huge megabanks have some big plans for how they are going to divide up America's wealth over the next decade. The scheme of the Lords of Money is that within a few years there be only *three central banks* that will control world currencies and thereby direct the entire world economy. Those three banks will be the Federal Reserve Bank, the European Central Bank, and the Central Bank of Japan.

Since the European currency and the Japanese yen are to become the world's two strongest currencies, the dollar will become the servant and workhorse of the world system. In other words, its strength is to be drained off and its value is to be diminished as the European and Japanese currencies grow stronger and more vibrant with each day. Eventually, there will be a money recall and all the world's currencies will be merged into one single world currency. Naturally, it will be necessary at that time, before the year 2000, to have one *World Central Bank.* Apparently, the International Monetary Fund will control this global banking system.

Noted researcher Salem Kirban, author of an insightful report, *The Coming One World Currency*, reveals that "The first priority... is to shut down the small banks, develop a conglomerate of a few huge banks... all united under one central bank. Thus, a World Central Bank!"[5]

Conspiratorial forces hope to close down most of the 13,000 commercial banks of the United States, converting most to branches of the few megabanks allowed to operate. To do this, they have secretly declared war against the smaller banks. That is why we see bank after bank closing its doors and the FDIC moving in to bail out depositors.

For Our Own Good?

The Order would have us believe that the consolidation of all our banks is a good thing. In *Business Week* magazine was an extraordinary editorial entitled "A Rare Chance to Streamline Banking." "Current troubles in the banking industry," said the magazine, "provide an important window of opportunity. They could help shore up the country's jerry-built banking system and give it the efficiencies to compete in a global banking environment. The banks' only economic function--borrowing capital and lending to businesses to facilitate commerce--must be consolidated."[6]

The unusual editorial in *Business Week* then went on

to describe exactly how the U.S. banking industry could be "reformed." "Here is how to do it," they said: "permit commercial banks to consolidate into a significantly smaller pool of players. Federal and state regulators should allow mergers and acquisitions of all banks, including big money center banks."

But that wasn't all, falling right into line with the plans of the megabankers and behind-the-scenes conspirators whom I call the Lords of Money, the magazine stated: "Reality also demands the *consolidation of government banking regulations* itself." In other words, the influential *Business Week* is calling for the regulation of all banks to be centralized and consolidated under *one giant super-regulatory agency.* Believe me, if this takes place, if one central regulatory agency is allowed to take the place of all of the various state and federal authorities, that consolidated agency will be controlled by the few megabanks that are still in existence at that time. Then they can run their affairs exactly the way they please with no one to even slap their wrists as is occasionally done today when the savings and loan and banking crooks and con artists loot and defraud millions of dollars.

According to the *New York Times*, the White House has bought into this scheme of consolidating all of the banks into the hands of just a few. According to the newspaper, "top officials at (the Department of the) Treasury have concluded that the banks should encourage creation of very large banks .... The excuse is a need to compete with large institutions in Japan and Europe."[7]

Globalist New Rules for Loans

Over the next few years, expect a gloomy future as this consolidation of banks proceeds unchecked. You will no longer be able to deal with someone you know in your home town when you wish to borrow. Instead you will probably sit down in front of the desk of an unknown bureaucrat of one of the giant megabanks who has been assigned to your local branch. Businessmen will be forced to go along with whatever conditions are placed on their operations in order to get loans so they can grow and compete.

Generally, if what they are doing does not fit in with the globalism goals of the conspirators, their loan applications will be turned down flat. Moreover, it can be expected that fundamentalist Christians, whether they be consumers or businessmen, will be left out in the cold by the new global money system and the internationalists who own our banks lock, stock, and barrel.

Meanwhile, global-minded New Age organizations and businesses will get the capital they need to grow and be able to outcompete the true, honest, patriotic business-men left in America today.

Bible Prophecy and the Control of Money

Bible prophecy indicates that all of society will be controlled in the last days through the money and currency system. The world of the Great Tribulation will be presided over by the Lords of Money using electronic systems to direct and control all commerce and business. In turn they will be required to pledge their allegiance to the one man selected to head the global, political and economic system: the World Leader (Revelation 13:16-17).

From my voluminous research I can say with authority that the process of consolidation of our banks and the destruction of the neighborhood banking system is already far advanced. In fact, I agree with one expert who has observed:

I believe every bank in a technical sense is in trouble. None of them are solvent. The Federal Deposit Insurance Corporation (FDIC) is the only thing that is propping them up, and they have enough money to protect only one percent of all the deposits.[8]

What is important for you to realize is that the handful of American megabanks have themselves already become the financial lackeys of foreigners who have no love for the American capitalist system, and as a matter of fact, despise our nation and its way of life. Remember, no longer is the United States the big kid on the block in terms of the global marketplace. What's more, the Lords of Money in Germany, Japan, Brussels, Paris, Geneva, and Basel, aided by their American accomplices, are able to manipulate our financial system, including the Federal Reserve, as if the American institutions were puppets on a string.

We are in debt up to our necks to the global moneymen. In the *Houston Chronicle* not long ago, the financial pages ran a series of special articles reporting on the economic summit held in that city by the Group of Seven, the leaders of the top seven Western nations. One of the writers asked a question that was especially poignant to our situation today. "What is it like being powerless in an economic world where all the decisions are made by the World Bank, the International Monetary Fund, and the huge trading partners?"[9]

The evidence is indisputable that this nation's central bank, the Federal Reserve, is sold out to the globalists. Notably, Lenin, the founder of communist Russia, once said, "a central bank is 90 percent of communizing a country."[10] In the radiant New International Economic Order planned for all of us by the elitists, the Federal Reserve Bank of the United States will be merged with and become subservient to an even greater central bank: the World Central Bank.

What to Look For...

The day the dollar dies what you will see first is that your local bank is suddenly closed. This will be done under the authority of the Monetary Control Act of 1980.

Next, you will be informed by the news media that the deposits of all banks have been frozen. It is possible to do this under Emergency Banking Regulation Number 1, 1961. But not to worry. Within a few days, the banks will reopen and, yes, they will have plenty of the New Money. In a slick con-job attempt, the government will assure you that your New Money will be good not only throughout the 50 states plus the territories of the United States of America, but throughout the world because it is being linked with all other currencies. The good news, you will be told, is that there is now an international currency.

Yes, it may have differences in design and esoteric symbols from country to country. But remember that little blank space, that white void I mentioned previously? You will notice in the new currency notes that there is a certain number, symbol, or mark within that space, or a picture of a man. Hold a bill to the light, and there you will see it. That is the sign, that is the indicator that this piece of paper will be convertible on the world currency exchanges. It doesn't matter whether you travel to Germany, Canada, Mexico, Jamaica, Brazil, or the Soviet Union, your money will be good. Or will it?

Houses And Autos Take The Plunge

In addition to the failure of our banks and savings & loans there is currently a depression in the real estate market. Rising home prices helped fuel consumer spending booms during the 60s and 70s. During the 80s, real estate in some markets of the economy, particularly in the northeast, in

New England and in California on the West coast, continued to skyrocket upward. But as 1990 rolled around, the sizzle had turned to pop and hiss. A real estate crunch has developed on the East coast and in New England, and prices on the West Coast in California have begun to stabilize and drop.

Incredible price increases in homes during prior decades made many Americans feel richer and richer. It was by borrowing on their mortgages that many yuppies were able to finance lifestyles far beyond their means. As a result, in the 1980s American homeowners tripled their consumer debt, doubled their mortgage debt, and halved their savings rate. But with home prices beginning to spiral downward in many parts of the country, homeowners are only now beginning to see the desperate financial shape which they are in. They realize now that this has been a big trap, and they are hopelessly mired in swamps of debt they cannot repay.[11]

As the price of homes has slid, and commercial real estate has gone begging, many American families have begun to realize that the good times could well be at an end. They can no longer depend on the price of their homes going up. This has affected their attitude about other purchases. It is why we see a plunge in auto sales developing.

For example, on August 15, 1990, it was reported that car and truck sales by U.S. companies had plunged 21.5 percent from year ago levels. Begged Chrysler Chairman Lee Iacocca, "Somebody start buying something in a hurry."[12] This is an early warning sign of severe economic problems. The more consumers refuse to buy durable goods--that is automobiles, refrigerators, furniture, and other large ticket items--the more a circular situation develops in which these industries are forced to lay off workers because of sagging sales. Then the vicious circle continues as those that are laid off are unable to buy goods. And so it goes until the nation sinks into depression.

You will notice that I use the word "depression"

rather than the milder "recession." The reason is that I believe the situation we will soon find ourselves in will be so desperate and so unbelievably shocking that even the word *depression* cannot truly describe its horrible dimensions. Even food, the most necessary resource of all, is not exempt from the effects of the coming depression.

Will Starvation Soon Plague America And The Globe?

During the late 70s and early 80s, there was a lot of ruckus about the plight of the farmers. You may recall that country singer Willie Nelson held a number of Farm Aid concerts attempting to raise money to keep the family farmer from going belly-up. Today, no one talks much about the farmers. What did happen to the family farmer, the guy who had only a few dozen acres? Why is the media silent?

The sad news is that most of the small farmers have left the farm and their families are now living in poverty. Cost of production forced most out of business. Farmers were forced to borrow huge sums of capital to operate and they built up insurmountable interest payments to the megabanks. As many as 85 percent of North American farmers have gone bankrupt in the last 15 years.

The shocking facts are that these farmers' land holdings were taken over by the government and the megabanks and sold off to what can be called the *super-farmers*, the *agri-businessmen*. These are defined as the producers with greater than $500,000 in gross income. These wealthy agricultural combines produce the vast majority of food today. Most are owned by rich men who do not personally work the land.

This corporate takeover of American farms by the rich means that agriculture is now in the hands of just a few. *The production and distribution of food has gradually been placed in the hands of the same men who control our money*

supply. This is frightening. It means that artificial shortages can be created instantly. There is almost an OPEC-
type cartel operating in agriculture today. A global food
crisis could be just around the corner with fast escalating
prices and total runaway inflation.[13]

Even the desperately poor third world nations such as
Ethiopia, Chad, Vietnam, and Peru are feeling the brunt
of the food crisis. As we move into the 1990s, news reports
indicate that world food aid shipments are at their lowest
volume since 1975-76, despite millions more people in dire
straights.[14]

These desperate people include those who live in one
of the world's strongest military nations, the Soviet Union.
Mikhail Gorbachev, their president, has been forced to go
to the United States and other Western nations begging
for massive new shipments of food to keep his bankrupt
communist government solvent.

Could it be that the leader of an impoverished Soviet
Union, with an angry and hungry population on his hands,
will someday soon decide to change his nation's economic
fortunes for the better by attacking in the Middle East
and capturing the oil rich lands of the Arab states? This
momentous event will no doubt occur. Why must it
happen? Necessity is one reason. Bible prophecy, however, is the major reason this invasion of the Middle East
by the Russian Bear is going to happen.

The Great Social Security Fraud

One of the most despicable gimmicks used by the White
House and Congress to cover up the huge federal budget
deficit is the looting of the Social Security Trust Fund.
For years, American citizens were told that the Social
Security Trust Fund needed shoring up, that the social
security taxes contributed by each American from wages,

salaries, and incomes had to be increased. So we saw a continuing round of increases until now we are figuratively paying out the nose for social security.

Unfortunately, this money may very well not be available to many of us when we grow old. The reason why is that at the same time we were told that we needed to shovel more money into the Social Security Trust Fund, Congress had opened the back door and was furiously shoveling the money out.

Where did the money go? It went to reduce the debt accumulated by the federal government for more than a decade.[15]

Since the government is broke, the budget schemers must shop around for where they can get money to pay the bills. Thus, in the budget for the current fiscal year, President Bush highly recommends that Congress continue to use what is called the "growing surplus in the Social Security Trust Fund." In reality, this trust fund is not in surplus at all. The money is spent almost as fast as it comes in.

Some of the money being stolen goes for the most abominable purposes. For example, the National Endowment for the Arts (NEA) was a beneficiary of some $175 million in the 1990 budget. The NEA is the governmental agency that promptly takes our hard-earned tax dollars and uses them to promote obscene art such as the Robert Mapplethorpe photographs glorifying child sexual abuse and so-called homosexual erotic art.

The NEA has also given taxpayer grants and monies to artists who have taken a simulated picture of Jesus, submerged it into a vat of urine, and called it art. One artist was given free money to depict Jesus as a heroin addict. Moreover, NEA money has gone to pornographic striptease artist Annie Sprinkles who did an "art show" in New York City in which she stripped completely and . . . well you get the picture.

What a national disgrace that our social security taxes have been doubled under President Reagan and Bush at the same time that millions of dollars are going for obscene, pornographic, ungodly art paid for courtesy of our local congressmen. Have you asked *your* congressmen and senators if *they* voted funds for the NEA?

America's Vital Signs Point to Disaster

As we have seen, a mysterious group of men pulling the world's financial strings have already succeeded in driving many banks and savings & loans over the cliff into oblivion. They are fast consolidating their financial and economic empire so that only *they* will control the printing and distribution of money. They already have a New Money in the works and are nearly ready to spring it on the American public. At the same time, they have been able to successfully grab hold of the reigns of our food production by driving tens of thousands of once proud farmers into bankruptcy and ruin.

These men have also engineered a secret takeover of American industry and real estate. They have devastated the real estate market, first driving up prices to dizzying levels, and then in some areas of the country selling off so fast that prices are spiralling downward. "Rock bottom" will be reached only when the titles to thousands of commercial properties they lust after fall into the laps of the conspirators. Consider the fact that even the prestigious Rockefeller Center in New York has been sold to the Japanese and you will understand what I mean. Further aggravating the coming financial crisis, our government has for years borrowed money from foreigners and stolen from the Social Security Fund to pay off staggering budget deficits.

All of the above are signs of impending disaster which point to the coming collapse of the money system, the subject we next examine.

NINE

The Coming Collapse of the Money System

Go to now, ye rich men, weep and howl for your miseries that shall come upon you. Your riches are corrupted, and your garments are motheaten. Your gold and silver is cankered; and the rust of them shall be a witness against you, and shall eat your flesh as it were fire. Ye have heaped treasure together for the last days.

(James 5:1-3)

The financial system of the free world is on the verge of a major catastrophe. In fact it almost collapsed in the summer of 1983 and the U.S. Government Printing Office was ready to print new money in case it did.

John Zajac
Delicate Balance:
Coming Catastrophic Changes of Planet Earth

The Lords of Money have decided that their dream of ruling the world can only be achieved through a cataclysmic financial crisis. When Paul said in I Timothy that the love of money is the root of all evil he certainly demonstrated the great wisdom given him by inspiration of God. It is this love for money and lust for power so as to control it that drives the money elitists on to their goals of world domination.

So what can they do to bring us under their complete and unchallenged control as soon as possible? The answer is crystal clear: give America, and indeed the entire world the *worst depression* ever in history. Destroy the savings and loans, and the banks, and cause a stock market bust that will make 1929's Wall Street crash look like a picnic. America is to be slaughtered financially, and the Lords of Money will then rise like a Phoenix from the ashes, debris, and carnage left behind on this continent.

Their plan is to make sure that the wealth of America falls into their hands to use for the glory of the new world they intend to create. In addition, a depression and economic chaos in America will result in this country totally surrendering to the world megabankers, thus creating the economic and financial opportunities inherent in a One World Order whose leadership will be doled out to the few at the top of the conspiratorial chain.

The Order's Version of Coming Events

If this sounds like too fantastic a scenario, I suggest you consider the sage advice of a few key people in the know. Norman A. Bailey is certainly one of those men. Bailey first joined Mobil Oil Corporation as an economist and then joined the Reagan administration as Director of Planning and Evaluation for the National Security Council. Later he was appointed Special Assistant to the President and Senior Director of International Economic Affairs at the White House.

Now consider what Norman Bailey had to say in a recent publication of the influential journal/magazine, *The World And I*. This journal is published by people high up in the Council on Foreign Relations (CFR). Bailey began by revealing some of the goings-on at a recent high-level international meeting of the elite:

> During a prematurely chilling, beautiful late September week in Washington, D.C., the cream of the world's commercial and investment bankers, national and international financial and monetary officials, economic journalists, and various hangers on, met at the annual International Monetary Fund-World Bank jamboree and congratulated themselves and each other.[1]

We see, then, that whether we call it a conspiracy or not, the fact is that the money men frequently meet together to plan strategy and tactics. True, Norman Bailey did not call this a conspiracy, but some of his terminology is quite revealing. For example, he jokingly (I assume) referred to the members of the famous G-7, the leaders of the seven top economic nations who meet annually in an economic summit, as "industrial mafia."

In his article, Bailey addressed the question of whether or not a financial cataclysm is imminent. Bailey, whose advice is often an indication of what those in The Order endorse, gave this answer:

> It can be argued that a very sharp deflationary collapse clearing the economic decks . . . is exactly what is needed, and that it would be most advantageous to the world economy in the long run.[2]

Bailey next reminded his readers that this is what the economist Schumpeter called "created destruction."

Bailey cites a number of reasons why there is likely to be a coming economic catastrophe. First, he summarizes the comments of former Federal Reserve Chairman Paul Volcker who observed:

> We are borrowing, as a nation, far more than we are willing to save internally. We are buying abroad much

more than we are able to sell. We reconcile borrowing
more than we save and buying more than we sell by piling
up debt abroad in amounts unparalleled in our history.[3]

According to Bailey, actions by the central bankers
over the past decade have "destroyed the underpinnings
of the House of Cards painstakingly built up..."[4] Therefore, he predicts, "the 1990s will begin with a severe
deflationary recession or depression, perhaps of a pro-
longed nature."[5]

Then came the propaganda designed to scare readers
and encourage them to see things the way The Order sees
them. Bailey suggested that even though another great
depression and financial crisis is almost certain, *the
nations should move now to organize themselves into a One
World Economic Order to insure that even though such a
calamity may occur, there will be "a reconstitution of a
meaningful international monetary system."*[6]

Following the coming great depression or recession
and after the "created destruction" has been achieved,
Bailey assures us that all of this financial wreckage:

> ...will be followed by the greatest boom in the history of
> mankind, so that the decade is likely to end in the midst of
> an expansion of unprecedented proportions. Those per-
> sons alive today who are still alive in the year 2000 will
> have difficulty recognizing the world...human life will
> have been transformed.[7]

When the Collapse Comes

Thus, we see the scenario which the schemers have in
mind for us. First, they will engineer a great financial
calamity. Our banks, savings and loans, and other financial
institutions will go down in flames (note that this process
has already begun), the stock market will fall off the cliff,

and a global money crunch will ensue. Then amidst the ashes will rise the glorious Phoenix; the New International Economic Order.

To let us know that all is well, the chosen World Leader will come forth to reassure the masses that an international task force is quickly putting the pieces back together. After this difficult journey through the valley of economic despair, he will tell us over worldwide TV linkup, the world will be a much brighter place. Over the following weeks he will go on television to tell us that a new World Central Bank will coordinate the world's financial transactions, that a commissioner has been appointed to oversee the various financial institutions around the world, and that a common currency will be issued. This New Money, he will add, will ensure that individual nation-states will no longer be able to tinker with the world's economy and generate such a crisis. Never again will there be such an economic calamity and a great depression. The world is in good hands now, he will say, misery is over.

Then, according to Bible prophecy, there will indeed be a period of great prosperity in the world for three-and-a-half years. In the midst of this unprecedented era of prosperity, the World Leader of the money elite will be so cocky and bold as to literally declare himself "God." It is at this point that all hell is going to break loose on planet earth with a great tribulation period of suffering and shame.

What would it take to set off an economic collapse, a great depression? As we have seen in the past, the stock market could well be the trigger. In October, 1987 when the stock market careened downward 508 points in a single session, we saw a foretaste of things to come. The collapse will no doubt occur almost overnight. As Howard Wachtel, an economics professor at American University has warned, "We could wake up one morning and find the situation out of control."[8]

Congressman Ron Paul warns that when the crunch does come, there won't be a shortage of money, it is just that money will have an astonishingly lesser value. "The real question is what happens when money will no longer buy anything? For example, someone receives a $500 check each month and they use it to pay their electric bill and don't have anything left with which to buy food. That is when the currency system collapses, and that is the potential during the next decade."[9]

John Zajac, former Vice President of Research and Development for such leading corporations as General Signal, Eaton, and Cutler-Hammer believes that the collapse could come through the banking system. He warns:

> If two percent of the banks close suddenly, the other 98 percent of the banks would also have a run and would have to close, causing all depositors to lose. Of course, if the banks collapse, the whole economy of the United States and the world would go into total turmoil. All financial markets would collapse with the banks.[10]

Zajac says that if the banks collapse, "the October 1987 stockmarket crash would seem mild by comparison."[11] Instead of losing 500 points (approximately one year's gain), the market could drop over 2000 points to a *level* of 500. As the New York and American exchanges fell, so would markets around the world. Confidence in America would diminish, causing foreigners to pull their deposits and investments from what was once the world's most stable country.

So the scenario we can expect is that one day suddenly a number of banks will begin to close their doors, setting off an avalanche of bank closures around the United States. The next day the casualties would mount as the financial toll is added up by the megabankers, the ones who will be keeping the books.

The failed bank assets would probably be worth next to nothing. A recent example of a failed banking system gives us a glimmer of the carnage. In December, 1988 the Revlon Corporation--strangely enough an international firm which specializes in cosmetics--bought a chain of failing Texas savings and loans which claimed $12 billion in assets. Revlon paid a paultry $300 million for these assets. That is less than three percent of their supposed value before the failure![12]

The Collapse Already Set in Motion

What few people understand is that the Lords of Money have already set in motion their plan for this incredible financial crisis to transpire. In 1980 they pushed through our Congress a major piece of legislation called the Monetary Control Act of 1980 (public law 96-221, March 31, 1980, Federal Register). That legislative act reduced the reserve requirements, the monies that banks and savings and loans are required to retain to insure solvency, to only three percent. Previously the financial institutions were required to carry a reserve of 100 percent!

A reserve of 100 percent means that the bank or savings and loan can only loan money deposited by customers or provided by owners of capital. This insures against default by the financial institution. However, with only a three percent reserve, *the banks and savings and loans can make loans of 33 times the amount the institution has on its books!* This shows how fraudulent is the entire Federal Reserve system. When our banks can lend out 33 times the amount they have in reserve, the foundation is laid for a major disaster.

This fact alone is scary enough, but now consider the next domino set to fall: The Federal Reserve supposedly has the capital to cover the three percent reserves in the system. But no one knows what the Federal Reserve Board does with the three percent reserves that are required. A handful of congressmen and senators have been calling for an audit of the Federal Reserve. In fact, there is now a bill pending in Congress (H.R. 844) which, if passed, would compel the Federal Reserve to open its books to public scrutiny. However, the elitist Board of Governors of the Federal Reserve are successfully resisting the passage of this legislation. The men at the top of this teeter-totter house of cards are not going to give us a peek at the rottenness that lies within their rickety structures.

Who Owns the Federal Reserve?

This all goes back to the question of who really owns the Federal Reserve? Very few Americans realize that the Federal Reserve is not a governmental agency and neither the Congress nor the President have one iota of control over its day-to-day operations. The chilling truth is that the Federal Reserve, America's central bank, is simply one component of an interlocking, international banking cartel that now controls the wealth of this planet.

William Greider, author of the provocative bestseller *Secrets of the Temple: How the Federal Reserve Runs the Country*, has said that the Federal Governors "have our fate in their hands." But, he explains, "have you read anything in the *Washington Post* who explains who *they* are?"[13]

What Greider is saying is that even the press appears mystified at how the Federal Reserve system operates and how it comes to its decisions which so vitally affect the American world economy. Greider notes that world financial markets react immediately whenever the Chairman of the Federal Reserve makes even what appears to be insignificant comments that might effect the economy. "Any tid-bit will do", he says, "and will cause reporters to run to their phone booth and start composing headlines."

Black Monday

To get an idea of how the collapse might begin, consider Black Monday. The day was Monday, October 19, 1987. It was the day the old financial order changed dramatically. On that day the Dow Jones Industrial Average plummeted by an astounding 508.32 points. The whole nation was alarmed. It was a "massacre," said one stock broker from Wall Street, interviewed on one of the news networks.

The Cable News Network (CNN) reporter told its audience of millions, "there was fear in the eyes of traders on the floor of the stock market today."

When the stock market closed on that fateful Black Monday, a dark cloud of gloom descended on the floor of the New York Exchange. Television reporters suggested that some investors would end up jumping out of windows just as they did after the shocking crash of the stock market in 1929.

The crash of October 19, 1987 was so unexpected that even those who had manipulated the stockmarket and engineered the crash were stunned. They had not yet put in place the mechanisms necessary to take over the world's stock markets and institute their New Money, their new one world currency. There is evidently still a number of details to be worked out. This shockwave of the DJIA bounding down by over 500 points caught these men unawares. To save their plan it was necessary that the Federal Reserve system pump emergency money into the market. A series of phone calls were therefore made that guaranteed the big banks and giant brokerage houses would not go under, that there would be money to support the market.

If it were not for these emergency phone calls the night of Monday, October 19, 1987, 47 million investors in the stock market would have lost almost everything they had. The ensuing money panic could well have caused unexpected repercussions and the World Leader the manipulators have chosen might not have been able to assume office. In fact, insurrections and revolutions might have broken out around the world as the peoples of the planet went crazy with fear and desperate apprehension.

It was apparent to all of the news networks as well as the various publishers of stock market advisory services that the leaders of the United States, Japan, Germany, Great Britain, France, and other nations and the officials at our Federal Reserve, the Deutschebank, the giant banks of Japan, and the Gnomes of Switzerland had kept the phone lines and the secret wires buzzing during the night. When the stock market opened on Tuesday, it was found that there was a sudden and unexpected infusion of money. The day was saved for the manipulators.

In the coming months, the Federal Reserve system created an astonishing amount of money and pumped many resources into the market to keep it from going under. The price, however, of this bailout is going to be severe. As investment analysts Abner Arbel and Albert Kaff explain in their book, *Crash: Ten Days in October... Will it Strike Again?:*

> The stock market crash in 1987 was far more severe than many people realize. During those ten days in October, more happened and happened faster, than ever before. But some of it is not yet known to the general public... the entire financial system of the United States came close to a complete meltdown... it was a narrow escape from disaster.[14]

Laying the Foundation

To fully take advantage of an economic crisis the manipulators behind the scenes must very carefully lay a proper foundation. This is very similar to the situation that Adolf Hitler faced when he took office in Germany in 1933. At first, the Nazi overlord was unprepared for a war with his enemies. It was necessary to stoke the fires of industry and build up a huge stockpile of bombs, aircraft, submarines, ships, tanks, armored vehicles, and other implements of war. It was also necessary to condition the German people, to raise their consciousness through propaganda. Various governmental institutions had to be set up, such as the dreaded Gestapo (SS), the propaganda ministry, and so forth. Plans for concentration camps had to be drawn up. The industrialists and bankers had to be drawn into the plot. All had to be ready to go when the whistle blew.

In 1939, Hitler felt that finally he was ready, and so his troops charged into action. This was the flashpoint that caused general declarations of war and resulted in over 50 million people dying in the flames of World War II.

Likewise, those who control the world's money supply are on the very threshold of seeing their fondest dreams come true. As my good friend Robert Faid has said in his bestselling book, *Gorbachev! Has the Real Antichrist Come?:* "The state of the world's economy is teetering on the verge of a catastrophic financial collapse." According to Faid, due to manipulations by the International Monetary Fund, the World Bank, international lenders, third world nations, and others, the international economy will soon come tumbling down.[15]

Repercussions After Black Monday

What has occurred in the years since the October, 1987 mini-crash of the stock market? First of all, the stock market, boosted by the money makers, began another great boom. The stock market had been rising since 1982. Now, it resumed the longest bull market upward in 50 years. Glad tidings were all around. No one seemed to understand how a world financial system teetering on disaster was able so quickly to overcome. The fact is, the stock market has been all glitter and very little substance. It is held together by the equivalent of bailing wire.

However, a wise financial commentator in the Italian newspaper *La Republica* wrote: "The crash is a prelude to... another phase in the cycle of American history. Black Monday will dredge up Roosevelt's ghost."[16] In Switzerland, the newspaper *Neue Zurcher Zeitung* suggested that the crash gave evidence of a "time bomb that has been ticking away for years."[17]

A South American newspaper wrote: "The brutal drop of the New York stock exchange offers difficult times for the world economy... we can expect international repercussions."[18]

In the few short years since the crash, little action has been taken to insure against a repeat. In fact, things are more dreary now than ever before. While our politicians promise us that the best is yet to come, and the stock market seems to be hitting on all eight cylinders, there is an underlying softness. Scrape past the external glitter and glamor of the economic miracle of the last decade and a surprisingly gloomy picture emerges.

We are very close to that moment in time when the economy will blow up. Billions of dollars will be lost by everyday Americans. Firms, corporations, and companies will close their doors on a colossal scale. The banking system will fail. The government will be unable to cope with this unparalleled disaster. The pain will be felt in the living room of the average American citizen.

Sadly, it may be too late to jar and jostle people and tell them "America, wake up!" The end is already in sight. What we must do as Christians is simply to hold on to our faith. He will pull us through even as others fall by the wayside in the coming days.

TEN

The Looting of America

*The rich ruleth over the poor and the borrower is the
servant of the lender.*

(Proverbs 22:7)

*As a result of the rapid rise in overseas debt since
1981, the United States has ceded considerable control
over its economy to foreign investors. They now hold
the power to help keep the U.S. economy growing or
help plunge it into recession. It would appear, in sum,
that President Bush will have to pay close heed to
their wishes . . . he has already felt the yoke of foreign
creditors.*

Wall Street Journal
December 5, 1988

The U.S. government, acting in concert
with the men who run the large international banks, has set in motion an
economic time bomb that will soon explode, sending
financial shockwaves to every corner of the globe. Let me
explain. You see, we have become the world's top debtor
nation, $3 trillion in debt. That is the number three fol-
lowed up by 12 zeros, $3 trillion. Incredible as this sounds,
it is unfortunately true. Federal deficits are higher now
than at any time in history. This year it approaches $300
billion. The deficit has tripled over the last decade.

Politicians have promised us lower spending year after year. They passed deceptive bills such as Gramm-Rudman, and said "we are going to cut spending and reduce this debilitating deficit." But the insiders know better. Politicians want to be re-elected. They will lie to be and we end up paying the bill for their lies.

Out of the colossal figure of $3 trillion in debt now owed, the commerce department reports that $664 billion of this money is owed to *foreigners*. We are going to pay for the hangover from our spending party, and that payoff is going to come very, very soon.[1]

The White House and Congress have played a shell game with our money. They continually use budget and accounting gimmicks to make the deficit look smaller than it is. Paul Blustein of the Washington Post Service very sagely wrote an article that was carried by many national newspapers entitled "Weaving a Web of Fiscal Deceit." "A huge sea of red ink," says Blustein, "separates budget rhetoric from substance."[2]

According to Blustein, "the government faces huge hidden costs in the future." This is why, although President Bush had pledged "read my lips, no new taxes," as 1990 began he reneged on that promise. We will indeed see new taxes. They are an absolute necessity because our government is not going broke, it *is* broke.

Debt by Design: The Invisible Hand at Work

How did the richest and most well-off nation in the world suddenly become the *top debtor?* How did we become so impoverished in such a short time? This could have occurred only through design. The masters at the Federal Reserve have certainly played their part in this fiery debacle. The Federal Reserve governors have used financial magic to create a financial explosion that will soon overtake the everyday man and woman on the street. Because the U.S. Congress keeps spending and spending money that it doesn't have, the Federal Reserve board continues to crank up the printing presses and print more and more. To do this, they must go overseas and borrow. Thus we see that the Japanese, the English, the Germans, and others have now bought so many treasury bonds that *these nations own America.*

Foreigners Now Own America

Foreigners now own America! That is what the influential *Wall Street Journal* intimated *several years ago* in 1988, as President Bush took office:

> As a result of the rapid rise in overseas debt since 1981, the United States has ceded considerable control over its economy to foreign investors. They now hold the power to help keep the U.S. economy growing or to help plunge it in recession. It would appear, in sum, that Mr. Bush will have to pay close heed to their wishes.[3]

Do you understand the implications of this? We are told by the number one financial journal in the world, the staid, conservative *Wall Street Journal*--the newspaper read and believed in by all the world's financial authorities--that our president will now have to do practically whatever the foreigners who own America tell him to do.

Have you wondered why when Saddam Hussein invaded Kuwait, it was America that was forced to spend hundreds of millions of dollars and put thousands of American soldiers lives on the line? Has it struck you as odd that rich nations such as Germany and Japan, who have used their billions of dollars and their massive wealth to buy up much of America, sat back on their haunches and did practically nothing during this crisis? Well, here is the reason: *they own us.*

It is very important that we again look at what the *Wall Street Journal* had to say: "They," that is foreigners, "now hold the power to help keep the U.S. economy growing or help plunge it into recession." This is an amazing admission. The masters of the financial world now have a stranglehold on your pocketbook and mine. They control us in every way except spiritual and they control most Americans in that respect, too. Economically they are our masters and they have made an obvious decision to wreck and ruin the American dollar. The White House and Congress are forced to go along.

Listen to what else the *Wall Street Journal* had to say:

> The massive pile up of debt has given foreign investors an ever increasing say in the economy's future. Their power was driven home to the president-elect soon after his election victory as the dollar dropped and interest rates began to rise. The episode, said former Federal Reserve Board Chairman Paul Volker was "a kind of warning that troubles lie ahead."

According to the *Wall Street Journal*, that warning was undoubtedly heeded by President Bush and his economic advisors, Secretary of State James Baker, Secretary of Treasury Nicholas Brady, and the Budget Director, Richard Darman:

> All three recognized the rising clout of foreign investors. Mr. Baker was whipsawed by the whims of international moneyflows during much of his tenure as Treasury Secretary and Mr. Brady concluded after his study of last October's (1987) market crash that Japanese investors triggered the debacle.

How startling! Our own Secretary of the Treasury is convinced that *"Japanese investors triggered the debacle"* of the 508 point plunge in the Dow Jones Industrial Average on October 19, 1987!

Worse, the *Wall Street Journal* continued, President Bush "may have little choice . . . he has already felt the yoke of foreign creditors."

This mind-warping news, that foreigners now have our president at their beck and call and that he is feeling their heavy "yoke," was reported on *page one* of the *Wall Street Journal* back in 1988. Now, several years later, the foreigners have an even tighter stranglehold and grip on the jugulars of our political leaders, on our economy, and on our dollar, our jobs, our salaries and wages, and our future.

Foreigners Buy Up U.S.A.

You may not realize it, but this nation no longer belongs to Americans. It is owned by the Germans and other Europeans, the Japanese, and by foreigners from such exotic locales as Taiwan, South Korea, Hong Kong, and Singapore. Everywhere we see evidence that America has been sold at bargain basement prices to the wealthy men who now control our destiny. Many of these men belong to such groups as the Carnegie Endowment for International Peace, the Council on Foreign Relations, the Trilateral Commission, the Bilderbergers, and other globalist groups. I believe there is every evidence that there is only a small, hidden clique of men who secretly influence all such organizations. These men are colluding together in the greatest scam since the days of Babylon.

In a recent issue of a journal called *Foreign Policy*, published by the Carnegie Endowment for International Peace, associate editor Thomas Olmstead wrote an article entitled "Selling off America." Olmstead's conclusions are startlingly accurate:

> Foreigners with fistfuls of devalued dollars now comb America for banks, businesses, factories, land, and securities. The result is a continuing erosion of control over decision making and technologies that are crucial to the creation of national wealth and power.[4]

Statistics show that foreigners now own 46 percent of the prime real estate in Los Angeles, 39 percent in Houston, and 33 percent in the nation's capitol of Washington, D.C. As one expert has noted, "Foreign purchases offer highly visible signs of America's declining position in the world economy and of the increasing penetration of its economic and political system by foreign interests."[5]

Our presidents have sought to reassure and calm Americans by proclaiming that the buy up of America is not really significant. Therefore, President Ronald Reagan suggested as far back as 1983 that "A world with strong foreign investment is good. We believe," said the president, that "there are only winners, no losers, and all participants gain from it."[6]

"Not so," responded Senator Frank Murkowski (Republican-Alaska). "Once they own your assets, they own you," said the blunt senator.[7]

"Today," said another authority, "America's heavy reliance on foreign capital . . . has greatly accelerated the decline of its global economic power. By 1986 nearly two-thirds of America's net investment in plants, equipment, and housing was being supplied by foreigners."[8]

The Great Buying Spree

The foreigners have bought up some of America's largest newspapers and publishing houses. They have even gobbled up many computer, high technology and military related firms. This puts our technological secrets and military technology in the hands of outsiders. Foreign lobbyists now roam the halls of Congress making payoffs and "large gifts" to congressmen who go along with their devious plans. These greedy outsiders do not love America, they love the color of money, and it does not matter what color the money is--green, blue, or pink.

Travel to any American city today, set your eyes on that city's largest buildings and realize this: those buildings could very well be owned by foreigners. By the year 2000, foreigners could own up to 75 percent of all of America's prime real estate. In New York City, they own the Rockefeller Center, the Tiffany building, and the Epson building. In Washington, the infamous Watergate Complex is owned by them. Our own Department of Justice is housed in buildings owned by foreigners. In Los Angeles, the huge Arco Plaza is in the hands of these outsiders.

Some 12.5 million acres of farmland in 49 states is owned by foreigners; they have controlling interest in up to one-third of our banks, and in the past year they have bought up over 500 companies in a variety of industries.

Who's Number One? Not America

After the flames of World War II had died to embers, such nations as France, Germany, and Japan began to rebuild. Now these nations are financial behemoths. In *Business Week* magazine, July 16, 1990, was listed the global 1000--the top 1,000 corporations in the world in terms of market value. Number one was Nippon Telegraph and Telephone, Japan's telephone and communications giant. This huge corporation is valued at over twice the worth of AT&T, but that is not all. The largest bank in the world is the Industrial Bank of Japan, valued at over $67 billion. The largest oil corporation in the world is not Gulf, Texaco, or Exxon. No, the largest is Royal Dutch/Shell, a combine owned by wealthy men in the Netherlands and Great Britain. General Motors is far outdone by Toyota in the auto business, while Ford Motor Company is lagging behind Germany's Daimler-Benz, which has put record numbers of Mercedes on America's freeways.[9]

How does all of this effect you? First of all, you should understand that these foreigners are even buying up Christian publishing companies. For example, one of the largest, Zondervan, is owned by Harper & Row, a secular publishing house which puts out unbelievably trashy materials. Harper & Row, in turn, is owned by the Australian magnate Rupert Murdock.

If you eat hamburgers at Hardee's fast food restaurants your dollars are going into foreign pockets. If you buy aspirin at People's Drug Stores, the same is true. Turn on the TV and watch such unholy shows as *The Simpsons* and *Married, With Children* on Fox Broadcasting Network and you are watching television programs owned by foreign interests. The clothing you wear may be from Brooks Brothers, owned by outsiders. And if you are a typist and use a Smith-Corona typewriter, be aware, it is built and marketed by foreign interests.[10]

The War On The Dollar

How has the international cartel centered overseas been able so easily to buy up most of America? The answer is simple. First, they made war on the dollar driving it down over 50 percent in value versus other major currencies in the last five years alone. Being able to get twice as many dollars in their hands, they then went on a shopping spree.[11] While the Japanese joined in what I call the Great American Flea Market Buying Spree, the real money masters are located in Europe, in Germany, Italy, Belgium, and Great Britain.

The Europeans who now rule the world have created a special form of money which they call the *Eurodollar*. This Eurodollar will soon be succeeded by a special currency distributed by the coming United States of Europe. But for now, the Eurodollar works just fine...if you're not an American! The giant banking interests in Europe have discovered that through the mechanism of the Eurodollar, they can buy up U.S. dollars at cheap rates and then use those dollars in turn to take over American resources.

Financial analyst Martin Mayer, in a very revealing article in the *Wall Street Journal*, recently reported on what he called the "evil and monstrous act" of the men who control the Eurodollar and have now bought up the major interest in America. Mayer noted that the London stock market had easily been manipulated by these men, but that what they have done to U.S. monetary sovereignty is far more severe.

"Because of the Euromarket," Mayer observes, "the U.S. lost control of its own money supply." In other words, our dollars have flown overseas and are now deposited in European banks, and European manipulators in turn use these cheaply bought dollars to buy up America. "These men," says Mayer, have in affect exported "their inflationary pressures to the U.S."[12]

The Storming of the Bastille

It is no wonder, then, that the infamous Council on Foreign Relations, in its journal called *Foreign Affairs*, has suggested that the United States will now "have to make painful adjustments."[13] Cryptically, the CFR remarked that when President Bush goes to Paris for the next economic summit it should be noted that the date is "the two hundredth anniversary of the storming of the Bastille."[14]

Predictably, according to the Council on Foreign Relations the only thing that America can now do given its state of economic distress, is to integrate its economy with the other world economies and thereby create one unified international system. This is a "painful process," say CFR insiders. "But it is essential if the trends toward economic integration among the world's market economies is to be maintained."[15]

Thus, we see revealed the brilliant plot of the conspirators: drive America to its knees financially and economically so that its people--you and I--will beg to be included in the New International Economic Order. After all, we don't want to be left at the station when the great United States of Europe train takes off. "All aboard! Get on now or else it will be too late!" comes the cry from the big boys. However, if we do jump on board, and I believe we already have, then don't be surprised if this turns out to be a nightmare ride on the Orient Express all the way to the fateful destination of Armageddon.

The Case Of The Vanishing Gold

It is now indisputable that America is under the yoke of a small but ruthless bunch of money manipulators. These men have destroyed the value of the dollar and have the ability to drive the United States to economic despair.

What would prevent us from just saying *no* to these wicked and influential men?

In years gone by we might have been able to do so. For one thing, we could have said, "Take your foreign currencies and get out of town by sundown. We still have our gold in Fort Knox." Gold, after all, has always been the preferred medium of exchange throughout the annals of human history. America is famed for its gold, a bonanza gleamed from the California gold rush and the great Klondike strike. In a sense, gold--or the lust for this precious metal--has made America the economic giant that it is today, or should I say *the giant it was yesterday.*

You see, our gold has vanished. "What?" you say. How could that be? Do we not have vaults brimming with gold bars at Fort Knox, Kentucky, protected by armed, uniformed U.S. soldiers? No, my friends. It is my sad duty to report to you that the gold has simply vanished.

No president since Franklin D. Roosevelt has personally seen any of the gold in Fort Knox. And, in fact, Roosevelt didn't see all of it. What an astonishing scandal of which every American needs to be informed! The gold at Fort Knox has been taken away and given to the Europeans. Now, if this sounds incredible to you, please read on and you will understand the mind-boggling truth about what has happened to our gold.

Because of American debt, the international money masters demanded and got our gold. It was drained through what is called the "London Gold Pool," an agency of the world's most powerful bank. It is now lodged deeply in the underground vaults of the Bank for International Settlements in Basil, Switzerland.

The Federal Reserve Board, in collusion with the Bank for International Settlements and the U.S. Treasury Department, has carried off one of the greatest thefts in the history of the world--the removal of tons of U.S. gold from bullion storehouses. There it sits secure in the hands of its European masters in 20 miles of tunnels in solid rock beneath the Alps of historically neutral Switzerland.

The Superbank That Now Has Our Gold

What is the Bank for International Settlements? This superbank was created in a series of economic planning conferences beginning at Brussels in 1920, and continuing in London, the Hague, Netherlands, and in Geneva. Our President Woodrow Wilson helped create the bank, and he was aided in his efforts by Aristide Briand, a former French prime minister who even back then was promoting a "United States of Europe." Briand and associates also secretly worked to promote a "New International Economic Order" and a "One World Government." Their plan was that the League of Nations, which later became defunct, could grow into this new world order.

To realize the new world order, of course, it was necessary to control the world's money supply. Thus, it was determined that the Bank for International Settlements would be established. It is literally beyond human explanation that this privately owned and secretly controlled bank could have our gold, and its leaders now have within their grasp all the money of this world. Only supernatural powers could have aided them in achieving their astonishing goal.

There are only a small number of U.S. congressmen aware of the great gold scandal. Recently, this handful of congressmen began to demand that the Federal Reserve be audited so it could be determined what has been done with this gold and how the Federal Reserve is manipulating our currency. Unfortunately, the Federal Reserve has stonewalled at every turn, and the White House has shunned all attempts to put pressure on the Federal Reserve.

It is clear that the influential men who run our money supply do not want to the truth to get out. If the American people fully understood what has happened to our vanishing gold, they would truly be up in arms. The great Boston Tea Party which instigated the American Revolution against the British would truly be a tea party compared with the armed rebellion that would confront the international bankers and their U.S. colleagues if this dirty little secret were to be discovered.[16]

Now that the international Lords of Money have all of our gold, there is literally nothing that we can do in terms of our own human powers to reverse the terrible situation that has been created. It will take God. God alone can overcome this situation. But as we read in the book of Daniel, certain prophetic events are predetermined by God (Daniel 11:36). They cannot be reversed. I am convinced that the vanishing of our gold and the centralization of all financial power in the hands of these few greedy men fits in with Revelation 13 and the coming of the beast of prophecy, the World Leader who will control all the world through its money supply. If it be God's will, all things will soon come to a climax.

ELEVEN

The New International Economic Order

*He is a proud man, neither keepeth at home, who
enlargeth his desire as hell, and is as death, and
cannot be satisfied, but gathereth unto him all
nations, and heapeth unto him all people.*

(Habakkuk 2:5)

*In the destruction of the old world order and in the
chaos of these modern times, the work of the new
creation is going forward.*

Alice Bailey
The New International Economic Order

The New International Economic Order is on the way. It has already hit the shores of America and it is gathering steam. When it hits with all the fullness of its fury it will move like a financial tidal wave, descending in a raging torrent over the unprepared. The New International Economic Order (NIEO) is being promoted from almost every quarter today, but it is the conspirators of The Order who are controlling the pace of this fast-growth movement.

President Ronald Reagan, claimed by Freemasonry as one of its own, heralded the coming of the NIEO in 1988 in a major speech in which he called for a one world system. A former member of the World Federalist Association, Reagan told his audience, "I want to talk to you about... the developing economy of the future, an economy of great challenges and even greater opportunities, if only we have the courage to embrace them... and open our arms to economic freedom on a world scale."[1] Reagan continued:

I speak of the economy of the future but it is forming now in the minds and imaginations of the entrepreneurs around the globe. It is... linked by a global network of investment and communications, it is transforming our lives so fast that the so-called conventional wisdom can barely keep up. But the dramatic changes we have already witnessed are only the foreshadowing of things to come.... We are moving to a new era of seemingly limitless horizons... this is good news for humanity.

Then Reagan made this stunning statement:

This new world economy is a *One World Economy*... a global electronic network, on line 24-hours a day... In this new world economy, national boundaries are increasingly becoming obsolete.

This was not the first time that Ronald Reagan had talked about a new One World Economy. His successor, George Bush, has been even more bold in declaring that a One World Economy has arrived and that the new system requires a different frame of mind, as well as new international machinery of control.

World Goodwill Takes the Lead

The brotherhood that makes up the money conspiracy, as we have seen, has many fronts. One of its chief propaganda mills is an organization called *World Goodwill*. World Goodwill is actually funded and run by the Lucis Trust, founded by a New Age occultist, the late Alice Bailey, and headquartered in London, Switzerland, and New York City. It is this same Lucis Trust that has revealed the existence of an undercover and highly secretive group who call themselves the *New Group of World Servers*. I believe this group is nothing more than The Order by another name.

In recent years World Goodwill has put forth a spate of papers, booklets and books, and has, in concert with the United Nations, their One World Order buddy, promoted numerous conferences and conclaves to promote the New International Economic Order. For example, one World Goodwill newsletter was entitled, "The Economic Problem: Finance, Trade and the Global Economy."[2] In this publication the masters of World Goodwill called for international cooperation for development. They noted that the United Nations Assembly has already put forth a detailed proposal for a New International Economic Order, and they advocated the rapid adoption of the United Nations proposals.

The principle that World Goodwill pushes the hardest is that called *Global Sharing*. This is simply a devious tactic designed to take from the middle classes and the working men and women of the world everything that they have earned and redistribute it to poorer countries. In reality, what is to take place is that the super-rich--those who now control our banking and money and own controlling interest in the multinational corporations that encircle the globe--will continue to hold on to their fabulous riches, property, and power. But the average American must sacrifice "for the good of all."

Chaos to Bring Forth New Order

The scheme put forth by World Goodwill was first announced back in September, 1980 in their 27-page publication entitled *The New International Economic Order*. The cornerstone of this new order, said World Goodwill, is that the old world order has to be *destroyed through chaos* so that a *new creation* can go forward. As Alice Bailey explained it:

> In the destruction of the old world order and in the chaos of these modern times, the work of the new creation is going forward; the task of reconstruction, leading to a complete reorganization of human living, and to a fresh real orientation of human thinking, is taking place.[3]

According to World Goodwill, "World economic relationships are now entering a new and more expansive phase, and this is occurring because the old order is no longer viable or productive and is in need of change." Continuing, the report stated, "The old order that had shaped the world until now is no longer adequate to meet the need." Therefore, "representatives of almost all the world's nation-states have agreed to discuss the creation of a new order among themselves."[4]

We know that in the recent past both President Bush of the United States and President Mikhail Gorbachev of the Soviet Union have parroted this line for a new world order. Gorbachev especially emphasizes *perestroika*, or reconstruction. Indeed, when the leaders of the two world superpowers met in Malta in 1989, the *New York Times* carried the headline, "Superpowers Forge New World Order."[5] Something frighteningly real is quickly coming to pass.

Sharing in The New Age

World Goodwill has also noted that man is moving into the "New Aquarian Age." And in this New Age, the attitude must be "the greatest good for the greatest number." In other words, here again we have the globalist plan to redistribute the world's wealth. Also keep in mind that the world's most wealthy men will not be required to contribute, only those middle class and working class people in the Western and other nations who will find that they have been reduced to serf and peon status by the controllers.

World Goodwill puts a happy face on their plan of sharing: "We're one humanity," reads their publication, "The distribution of the world's wealth will be more equitable. The life-sustaining energy of money will find freer circulation and more productive use."

What a deceitful lie! Take away your money, give it to others, let the rich, upper-class few keep their wealth, and the whole world will be better off.

The publication entitled *The New International Economic Order* also announced that tremendous spiritual changes had taken place in the world, resulting in a "new global consciousness."[6] This is why it is possible, said the publication, that the New Order could be founded with the understanding that men are "at different stages of evolutionary development."[7] If men are at different stages of evolutionary development, then naturally some, in the New Age view, would already be *god-men*. God-men have supposedly attained an evolutionary state or stage of development in which they possess something the New Agers call "Christ-consciousness," or "global consciousness. These are the men who are slated to become the imperial magistrates of the New World Order. These it will be who oversee the distribution of the world's wealth and resources. You better believe that most of it will end up in their pockets.

World Unification the Goal

The real purpose of the World Goodwill campaign is world unification. In fact, they are quite frank about it. "The NIEO is a call for unification." Now is the time to get rid of "negativism and divisiveness."[8] A patriotic American who believes that the nation's borders should not be erased and dissolved and who still feels that the American dollar should be worth more than the paper it is printed on obviously will be considered one of these negative and divisive creatures who will have to be dealt with if the New International Economic Order is to come into being. After all, in the New Age view, such a person has not evolved properly into the godlike estate now held by the masters who pull the strings of World Goodwill.

The Ten Kingdoms of the New Order

Another internationalist group with a New Age vision busily promoting the New International Economic Order is the *Club of Rome*. In Bible prophecy we see that Revelation 17 clearly reveals that there will be ten great world rulers, heads of nations or groups of nations, in the last days who will give their strength and power unto the beast. These will be *of one mind*, says Revelation. It is not so amazing, then, to discover that the Club of Rome, whose membership is comprised of some of the world's most influential and wealthy men, has a plan for a New World Order in which all of the world's nations will be placed within ten groupings. The first three groups are the most powerful and these are the very same groups promoted by the Trilateral Commission.

First is North America, made up of Canada and the United States of America. Group Two is Western Europe, which will be led by Germany. Group Three is Japan. The other groups include Latin America, Eastern Europe, North Africa and the Middle East, Main Africa, South and Southeast Asia, and Centrally Planned Asia. It is intended that amidst a coming world financial panic and crisis, the peoples of the world will cry out for a World Leader to come and bring order out of chaos and end the misery and despair caused by the world financial breakdown. At that point the proposal for the ten groups, or kingdoms, will be used as the blueprint for world domination by The Order.

The Phoenix Takes Flight

The New International Economic Order can only be realized if the plan for a *world currency system* is also realized. The dollar will have to go. To accomplish this, the Lords of Money must pave the way administratively and through propaganda--preparing the world psychologically for what is going to be a very traumatic change.

A shocking example of this propaganda campaign to condition us was the publication by one of Great Britain's top financial magazines, *The Economist*, of a feature article entitled "Get Ready for a World Currency." On the front cover of the monthly magazine was a picture of a Phoenix bird rising from the burning ashes of all the world currencies. About the Phoenix bird's neck was a chain and on it a gold coin, printed with the words "Ten Phoenix."[9]

In the magazine article itself, the publishers of *The Economist* made plain that only a world currency could solve the world's growing financial crisis. Thus, dollars, pesos, lira and other currencies would be replaced by a new currency called the *Phoenix*. Let me quote from the opening paragraph of the cover article:

Americans, Japanese, Europeans, and people in many
other rich countries, and some relatively poor ones, will
probably be paying for their shopping with the same
currency. Prices will not be quoted by dollars, yen, or
deutschemark, but in, let's say, the Phoenix. The Phoenix
will be favored by companies and shoppers because it will
be more convenient than today's currencies, which by then
will seem a quaint cause of much disruption to economic
life in the late 20th century.[10]

Significantly, the author of this article writes that the
dollar has gone up and down in value like a rollercoaster
over the last ten years or so. It will not be long, he says,
before "it will collapse." But the solution is at hand.
"Pencil in the Phoenix," he cheerily recommends, "and
welcome it when it comes."

It is quite likely, then, that the new currency that we
will be using at some point in the near future will be called
the *Phoenix*. There is a reason for this. To the ancient
Egyptians, the Phoenix represented the Phoenician God
"Phoenix" as well as their own deity who was described as
"Vanu." The spirit of this deity is a phallic symbol. The
Egyptians and the Phoenicians taught that the god represented by the Phoenix bird "rose to heaven in the form of
a morning star, like Lucifer, after his fire-immolation of
death and rebirth."[11]

According to Barbara Walker, author of *The Women's
Encyclopedia of Myths and Secrets*, the god represented by
the Phoenix was the sacred king cremated and reborn.
When an ancient pharaoh or king died and was cremated,
his soul was supposedly released above the fire and, as it
arose, it assumed bird form. That bird, according to
Egyptians, was the Horus Hawk, closely associated with
the Phoenix. Horus is also known as the *All Seeing Eye* of
the Pyramid (see the reverse side of the Great Seal on the
U.S. one dollar bill!).[12]

The Phoenix bird pictured on the front cover of *The
Economist* was crowned with the *fleur de lis*. The fleur de

lis has long been the symbol of French royalty; therefore, the artist and those in the know at the magazine were perhaps telling us that it would be the United States of Europe and its central bank that will control this new international currency.

However, I believe there is yet another reason why the fleur de lis was chosen to crown the Phoenix. The fleur de lis was said to picture the *Iris* blossom. Iris, in turn, was the name of the Greek goddess of the rainbow. It is possibly as an Iris blossom that the true meaning of this fleur de lis comes clearly into view.

In Crystal City, Virginia, is headquartered a company called *International Reporting Information Systems (IRIS)*. IRIS is a computer information gathering, storing, and retrieval service which claims it will rival the Central Intelligence Agency (CIA) in the ability to gather and supply *global financial information* to governments and businesses.[13]

Backed by a number of large European financial institutions, IRIS reportedly has financial correspondents and agents around the world and a large technical and administrative staff. Its system includes a massive computer equipped to handle unlimited amounts of information--financial and otherwise--on almost any subject. Robert McNamara, former president of the World Bank and reportedly also a member of the Lucis Trust, is only one top official who has endorsed the IRIS system.

What is fascinating about IRIS is its location in Crystal City, Virginia, not only because the New Age promotes an esoteric belief in the energy powers of crystals, but because the town is just a few miles from CIA headquarters!

According to the *Multinational Monitor*, IRIS has an "international advisory council" headed by former British Prime Minister Edward Heath. Its membership includes McNamara, former French Minister of Commerce Jean-Francois Deniau, representing Europe, and former Columbian Finance Minister Rodrigo Botero, representing South America.[14]

It is therefore possible that *The Economist*, which is published both in London and New York, was signaling its elite members that preparations continue for the New World Currency and that not only will the currency be controlled by the financial cartel in Europe, but it will be electronically supervised by the tremendously powerful IRIS computer system in Crystal City, Virginia.

The Use of Occult Symbology

The men who plan to rule the world often operate using occult principles, terminology, and symbols which, to the uninitiated, appear to be either absurd or curiously irrelevant. Things like the *fleur de lis* symbol atop the head of a *Phoenix bird* and the naming of a company *IRIS* in the town of *Crystal City* may appear somewhat ridiculous to you or me. But to the men of The Order, trained and schooled as they are in the more arcane teachings of the mysteries of the occult, these things contain profound meanings.

Such symbols and terms hearken back to the days of the Mystery Religion of ancient Babylon, Greece, and Rome. Indeed, in a spiritual sense, the present conspiracy first began in Rome and Babylon. Ironically, as we shall see in the following chapter, the conspiracy is destined to return to these same evil roots. A "New Rome" is on the immediate horizon.

PART THREE

The Empire Strikes Back

TWELVE

The New Rome and the Resurrection of Hitler's Ghost

*And in his estate shall stand up a vile person ... he
shall work deceitfully for he shall come up, and shall
become strong with a small (few) people.*
(Daniel 11:21, 23)

*It is necessary that I should die for my people; but my
spirit will rise from the grave, and the world will know
that I was right.*

Adolf Hitler
Hitler's Last Testament

I s the bloodthirsty spirit of Nazi warlord
Adolf Hitler about to be resurrected?
Will Germany once again go on the
march and plunge the entire world into flames? I believe
the startling answer to these questions, regrettably, is yes.

Hitler himself, in his Last Testament, on February 25,
1945, dictated this message:

The task I have undertaken as raising the German people
to the place in the world that is their due is unfortunately
not a task that can be accomplished by a single man or in a

single generation. But I have at least opened their eyes to their inherent greatness and I have inspired them to exaltation of the thought of the union of Germans in one indestructible Reich. I have sown the good seed.[1]

Contrary to his claim of "good seed," the seed that Hitler had sown produced a bitter harvest, as any recounting of Nazi history reveals.

It is a loathesome thought that the new united Germany could inherit the same spirit of evil that resulted in widespread massacres of six million people in concentration camps and as many as 50 million in the fires of World War II. The last words of a nonrepentent Hitler are reputed to be this thought-provoking boast: "It is necessary that I should die for my people; but my spirit will rise from the grave and the world will know that I was right."[2]

The Resurrection of Hitler's Ghost

There are forces today in this world who are working furiously to resurrect Hitler's ghost from the ruins and debris of the past World War. The Lucis Trust, a top New Age and globalist organization with a worldwide network, refers approvingly to Hitler in one of its publications with the assertion that "there was an attempt by a disciple to unite Europe along the lines of the Rhine River." According to the publication, that attempt failed but it will be tried again![3]

Another New Age authority, Benjamin Creme, admiringly reminisces about Germany. He writes, "The German racial strain is ancient, but the nation is young, astral, and mediumistic, and therefore responded readily to the powerful first ray force, materialistically hopeless, of its dictator Hitler (a medium himself), and Bismarck."[4]

Creme adds that Germany's national motto is "I preserve." This is, he says, Germany's *esoteric* motto. It therefore indicates that the Satanic hierarchy believes Germany's future role to be that of preservation of the great mysteries of Babylon, the revival of world domination by Rome, and the uplifting of the superior race of god-men.

Watch Out for 1993?

In studying occult numerology recently so that I could attempt to grasp the twisted and perverted reasoning of those involved in the occult conspiracy, I came upon an interesting and quite revealing configuration of numbers. Adolf Hitler assumed power in Germany in 1933. The number 33 is extremely important to the occultists. Jesus was crucified on the cross at the age of 33. In Freemasonry, the 33rd degree is the highest to which a man can attain. Adding the digits *three* plus *three* in the number 33 gives us the sum of *six*, which to Christians is a most unholy number (see Revelation 13 where the beast is described as the man with the number 666). But to the occultist and New Age mind, *six* is a supremely *holy number*.

Three is also an important number to occultists because of their belief in an unholy trinity of a father of light; his mistress, the goddess; and their offspring or son, who is pictured as the "Messiah" or "Christ" of earth, being of course a counterfeit of the *true* Messiah Jesus Christ.

Nine is also an important number from an occultic, numerological standpoint because *three* times *three* equals *nine*. Witches were once claimed to have *nine* lives. In ancient Greco-Roman mythology there were said to be *nine* archons or lords who ruled planet earth.

The occultists would propose that Hitler's assumption to power in the year *33* was a great occultic event. They note also that exactly *six* years later, Hitler invaded Poland and plunged the world into a fiery war to attain the aims of his master.

The startling fact is that since post-war history has now revealed that Hitler was an occultic member of a Satanic secret society called the Thule Society, it is entirely possible that Hitler's Germany chose the date of 1939 to invade Poland, kicking off World War II, simply because of these two occult factors: (1) *1939* was exactly *six* years after Hitler rose to power, and (2) the number *39* itself contains an esoteric message.

In unraveling the meaning of the number 39, we first realize that in Satanic teachings we find the dictum that *truth is reversed.* Thus, in the bizarre world of occultism, if Hitler initiated a quest in 1939 to take over the world, crush Jews and Christians, and reign in favor of his master, Satan--and this attempt failed, *then another attempt should be tried in the year 93 (1993)--exactly the reverse of 39!*

Now again, I well recognize that all of this is so much nonsense and absurdity. But whether we see numerology as weird and ridiculous or not, the fact is that some of the most powerful and influential men in the world today-- men who sit at the very helm of governments in Europe and control much of today's world banking and inter- national commerce--*do believe* in an occult numerology. Therefore, their actions are often based on this doctrinal belief.

Thus we see that the New Age Movement conducted its World Harmonic Convergence on August 16/17, 1987. Weird though it may be, to the occultists this indicated *16* going on *17* (the event was held during both the 16th and 17th of August). Adding the digits *one* and *six* produces seven, and the sum of *one* and *seven* gives us *eight.* Thus, the occult message of the Harmonic Convergence was that we are going from God's era (the perfect number of *seven*) to their master Lucifer's era (which is symbolized by the number *eight*, the number of the "new beginning" after the old order of God--seven--is destroyed).

Jose Arguelles, the mastermind of the Harmonic Convergence, repeatedly said that the date of this celebration was chosen *based solely on pagan prophecies.* Counting *six years after* 1987, we come up with the year *1993.* Here again we see the number 93, which fits in with the goals of the occultists.

The Year 1993 Just Keeps Popping Up

Another clue to the plans of the occultists comes from the dark, twisted writings of the British satanist Aleister Crowley, a contemporary of Adolf Hitler. Crowley claimed that Horus, the War God (also pictured as the eye on the triangle atop the pyramid on the U.S.'s one dollar bill!), had given him a vision of war and vengeance. Horus had told Crowley "I am the Warrior Lord of the 40s."[6] Now it is significant that Crowley wrote of his vision from Horus in the year 1904--almost four decades *prior* to the bloody 40s of World War II and at a time when the majority held the opinion that war had been banished from civilized nations altogether.

Crowley also was led to believe--and he revealed in his Satanic text, *The Book of The Law*--that the most significant number in the occult world is *93.*

Robert Anton Wilson, a writer sympathetic with occult views, explains in his book, *Cosmic Trigger,* that "93 is also the cabalistic numeration of the word *phelema*, the "'Word' of the New Age." According to Wilson, this magical word phelema comes with a motto: "Do what thou wilt." Significantly, in his *The Book of The Law*, Aleister Crowley gives this as *the* great commandment of all Satanists: "Do what thou wilt shall be the whole of the law."[7]

What does all this mean? Simply that what the

occultists call the "Great Work," the illumination of all humanity, is supposedly to be accomplished in the year *1993*, a year which will see the ascension of a New World Order and a universal religion built on New Age tenets.

We should, of course, keep in mind that although the occultists may believe that 1993 is their big year, the year when they will reach the pinnacle of success and finally control the whole world for their master, the true God of this universe may have quite different plans. We operate not on Satan's timetable, but that of God Almighty.

Therefore, the year 1993 may well pass us by with nothing of significance occurring. However, if it be God's will that He allow these things to transpire, then 1993 could be a very significant, key year. It could even begin the Great Tribulation period, to be followed in the year 2000 by the return of Christ to set up His 1000 year millennial reign. Again, I emphasize, I do not state this as fact, but merely a possibility. All depends on the Will of God.

We cannot know for sure the day nor the hour of our Lord's return. Yet, it would be wise of us to realize what Satan has in mind, "Lest Satan should get an advantage of us: for we are not ignorant of his devices" (II Corinthians 2:11). Many of the events we see going on around us in the financial, educational, religious, and political realms are based on Satan's agenda and his timetable.

Frankly, I do not believe that the year 2000 will see the return of Christ. It could happen *before* that date. God has a way of confounding our expectations. He is, after all, God, and He does what He wants, a fact of which we should all be most appreciative and grateful for it indicates the depth of His incomparable power.

A United States of Europe by 1993?

In this light, it is an amazing thing that the coming United States of Europe, according to an article in the *New York*

Times, is "likely to be completed by *1993*." The *Times* story confided that:

> Top European policy makers have quietly warned the Bush Administration that the economic and political integration of Europe is moving far more rapidly than had been expected, a development that could have important implications for U.S.-European relations.[8]

According to current plans, the United States of Europe will in 1992 first unify commerce and trade. All national borders will be dissolved in respect of trade between nations. Then following this development, economic and then political union is to take place. A form of European currency is already being used today and is called the European Currency Unit (ECU).

The United States of Europe is initially to be made up of the twelve nation-states of the European community. There has already been developed a flag of twelve stars against a blue field and even a national anthem which will be based on Beethoven's "Ode to Joy." There is also a tentative European parliament in place. This incredible political-economic development, the creation of a confederation of European states, to be known as the *United States of Europe*, is an incredible fulfillment of Bible prophecy. It is nothing less than the revival of the once great Roman Empire.

A Fourth Reich?

The most powerful nation among the twelve nation-states which comprise the European Community is without a doubt a united Germany. Will this ascension of the new Germany--united, powerful, determined, and assertive--result in a *Fourth Reich?*

There can be little doubt that Germany will dominate the United States of Europe. In fact, Germany already dominates Europe. We can only come to this mind-boggling conclusion: What Hitler failed to achieve through bombs and armament, the new Germany has achieved through the power of money!

I am not alone in my conclusion. In the conservative and highly respected *Wall Street Journal* of July 13, 1990 was a report that one of the most prominent leaders in Great Britain today has come to the same alarming conclusion about Germany. His name is Nicholas Ridley, and until recently he was Britain's Trade and Industry Secretary. This is somewhat the equivalent of combining both the Department of Commerce and the Department of Labor into one job here in America.

Nicholas Ridley stirred a political whirlwind with a strident attack on the European Economic Community and particularly West Germany. He warned that a United States of Europe led by Germany could prove a disaster. Known as a close political ally of Britain's Prime Minister Margaret Thatcher, Ridley gave his views in a sensational interview by the *Spectator* magazine. Here is what he had to say:

Number One. According to Secretary Ridley, plans for a European Monetary Union are "all a German racket design to take over the whole of Europe. It has to be thwarted." Ridley further commented: "This rush take-over by the Germans, on the worst possible basis, shows the French behaving like poodles to the Germans, and is absolutely intolerable."

Number Two. Ridley warns that Germany is becoming "uppity" and claims that Germany is "already running most of the European community."

Number Three. The British trade and industry overseer remarked that the European Community Commission in Brussels, Belgium, consists of "17 un-elected, reject politicians with no accountability to anybody... who are pandered to by a supine (weakling) parliament."

Number Four. Secretary Ridley asserted: "I am not against giving up sovereignty to the European Community in principle, but not to this lot. You might just as well give us Adolf Hitler, frankly."

When the opposing politicians and business leaders, including the president of one of Germany's largest banks, the Bundesbank, protested that Ridley's comments could cause "a bloody revolution," Prime Minister Thatcher was forced to remove Ridley from his job as Trade and Industry Secretary. Still, it is suspected that Thatcher also has great doubts about Britain's entry into the European Community (soon to be the United States of Europe), and it is believed that she is secretly in sympathy with Ridley's comments. Nevertheless, England is being forced, by economic threat and financial blackmail, to go along with plans for the new United States of Europe.

"A Specter is Haunting Europe"

Perhaps we should pay heed to Nicholas Ridley's frightening advice to the world. West Germany, he predicted, "will soon be trying to take over *everything.*" Many political leaders around the globe echo Ridley's view. In a prestigious American journal, *The Wilson Quarterly,* political analyst Steven Lagerfeld contributed an article entitled "Europhoria." "A specter is haunting Europe--the specter of 1992," wrote Lagerfeld.

Lagerfeld referred to 1992, the date in which the United States of Europe will formally and tentatively become one nation. Within a few short years after that, there will be monetary union and no doubt a common currency. Once monetary union is achieved, we will see a total oneness in the political and military realm as well. Political and military power inevitably follow the trail of money.

The German mark is fast becoming *the* currency of choice in the world economy. The U.S. dollar weakens daily and the Soviet Ruble is a joke in world trade circles. But the mark is king! Thus, as the Soviet Union's pitiful economy collapses to the ground, Gorbachev is forced to go to Germany's money men (The Order) and beg for marks to prop up his sagging economy. Meanwhile, America sinks into a morass of debt and the dollar falls to new lows. In Germany, then, we see the shape of the future. The Phoenix has taken flight!

Germany is on its way to becoming the unchallenged powerhouse of the globe by the year 2000. In a commentary in the Australian newspaper, *The Age*, in April, 1990, Peter Smark wrote, "We are on the brink of a German century and accommodating to that will be painful and difficult for many countries." Smark also observed that "It is incontrovertible that Germany's power and influence are growing daily."

What Does Germany Want?

Should we fear the on-rushing German juggernaut? Should we heed the words of Sir Winston Churchill who once gave a speech, in which he observed: "The Germans are either at your feet or at your throat."

What does Germany really want to accomplish? What will this nation do once it is united and a new chancellor takes office to lead what is becoming the most powerful nation on earth? Recently, I talked with a good friend of mine, Joseph Carr, author of the insightful *The Twisted Cross*, the story of Hitler's occultic Nazi regime. "The Nazi era is not necessarily over," Carr told me. "The same forces that existed then have not been extinguished entirely."

Then, in *Foreign Affairs Journal* recently (Winter 1989/1990), was this insightful analysis: "The authoritarian traditions and structures that allowed Nazism to flourish were never fully eradicated." Moreover, the author believes that "the Germans are at the center---and are determined to press their advantage."

Bestselling Christian author and attorney Constance Cumbey, in her excellent, groundbreaking book unmasking the New Age Movement, *The Hidden Dangers of The Rainbow,* has a stunning chapter on the Nazi-New Age link.[9] She proves that without a shred of doubt, the ghosts of the past are active today in the widespread New Age Movement, a system of occultism destined, it appears, to transform the world's religious and political structures. The New Age is in fact the vehicle seized on by The Order to fulfill many of its most cherished objectives.

The Future of A United Germany

Amazing events are taking place today in Germany. Who could have suspected that the Berlin Wall would come tumbling down so soon? Who other than God could have envisioned that the German people in Berlin would mingle among themselves in the streets, arm-in-arm, crying out, "Give us a united Germany!"

Some are frightened of the prospect of a united Germany. Could a reunited Germany bring about a Fourth Reich? Is it possible that the fires of World War II could be reignited? One Czechoslovakian leader was quoted in the *New York Times* as saying:

> All of Germany's neighbors have got to be against reunification. Once East and West Germany have been unified, what is to stop the Germans from wanting to get back all their old lands in the east, from Pomerania [part of Poland] to Silesia [southwest Poland] and the Sudetenland [Czechoslovakia].

There is much fear in the thought of a reunited Germany, and I believe the rapture clock is ticking away today.

Helmut Kohl said of the German nation:

> We belong together, and no matter how long it will take, in the end we will achieve the unity and the freedom of Germany.

I don't question West German Chancellor Helmut Kohl's motives. But unwittingly he is following a blueprint drawn up by dark forces. In *Maitreya's Mission*, Mr. Creme says that his spirit guide, the master Djwhal Khul, has prophesied that:

> Germany will again give to the world the blueprint of a correct (that is spiritually-oriented) hierarchical form of government.[10]

Adolf Hitler's Nazi Germany offered a blueprint of a hierarchical form of government, and now a demon master is telling this New Age leader it is going to happen *again*.

Isn't it interesting that even a New Age demon spirit knows that Germany's blueprint for the world will again be put into action very soon? Can we trust lying demon spirits? I think not, and I wouldn't give any of this any credence at all if it weren't for the Bible prophesying a great revival of the Roman Empire. Revelation 13 describes a beast with seven heads and ten horns, with ten crowns, which are ten kings or kingdoms in the last days. Will they ascend out of a reunited Germany, this great economic power rising like a Phoenix bird from the ashes of World War II? Has the wound of the beast been healed? Will Germany head up the *New Rome?*

Anti-Semitism Spreads in Germany

Other unusual and incredible developments have recently begun to transpire. The growth of anti-Semitism, a hatred of Jews, is again spreading throughout Germany. Who is causing this? What kind of horror is being raised up in people? The *Washington Post* news service, in a report from Berlin, states:

> Vandalism, death threats, and public demonstrations by neo-Nazis have led East Germany to warn against the rise of neo-fascist groups.

There are also reports that the neo-Nazis want to have a Fourth Reich in a united Germany. That should frighten those who don't know Jesus Christ and yet are wondering what is happening in the world today.

In a recent edition of the *Washington Post,* political columnist George Will wrote that *perestroika* was the foreign word given the widest usage in the 1980s, but in the 1990s there will be a German word that is coined and used: *Anschluss*. In essence Anschluss means "German land for German people." If the 1980s was a decade of triumph for freedom, the 1990s could possibly be a decade of tragedy for the cause of freedom. The dark side of Eastern Europe and Russia could be revealed.

We Want a Fourth Reich!

Recently, as the world viewed the spectacle of the fall of the Berlin Wall, West Germany's Chancellor Helmut Kohl went to Berlin to speak to a combined crowd of East and West Berliners. As he commenced his speech and started to discuss the reunification of East and West Germany, a determined group of listeners began to cry out, "We want a Fourth Reich!" How startling! Hitler boasted that his Third Reich would last for a thousand years. Instead it lasted 12 years and killed 50 million! Now some Germans have already forgotten the past and are again eager for a new Reich.

Many Europeans are worried about all of this but incorrectly imagine that the new United States of Europe will submerge Germany within its borders. Rather than having a reunited German juggernaut with Germany controlling the continent, these observers mistakenly suppose that the United States of Europe will diminish the power of Germany acting alone.

The fact is, of all the European countries, the greatest force of all would be a united Germany, and that powerful, unified nation could and will *dominate* all of Europe. Hitler attempted to conquer Europe with armed might. The coming Fuhrer will seize all of Europe without a shot being fired! Then, following the blueprint of The Order, Germany and the United States of Europe will put together a One World Order. This will be the fulfillment of Revelation 17 and Daniel 2:40, the revival in the last days of the great Roman Empire/Mystery Babylon international confederation.

This is a frightening prospect for those who do not know God's Word. But from Bible prophecy we know how it's going to end. There will be many shocked people, but God's children will not be among them. We who know Him view the future with confidence as we place our trust in God's control and in His Plan.

The Failed Boast of an Arrogant Dictator

Hitler once bragged, *"Jesus Christ failed, whereas I became chancellor."* How desolate must have been the last days of this Satan-driven German warlord as, hidden deep beneath the earth in his bunker, he could hear the frightening screeches of war overhead. He had failed in his quest to become world sovereign. His plan for a millennium of German superiority was crushed. So, Adolf Hitler put a pistol inside his mouth...and pulled the trigger.

In contrast, consider Jesus' incomparable achievement. The Bible says that Jesus came to destroy the works of the devil, and He did so on the cross. Moreover, even the grave could not contain Him. He rose on the third day of His own will! Victorious forevermore!

The Fourth Reich and The New Rome

What we can look for, then, is the birth of the new Fourth Reich which will be the United States of Europe with Germany and its political leader sitting on the throne. This is the result The Order has worked centuries to achieve. This is the dreaded spectacle of the *New Rome,* the beast that was wounded, yet has come back to emerge again as a vibrant world force (Revelation 13). Since Bible prophecy has so much to say about this revival of a New Rome in the last days, it is important that we take a look at this astonishing turn of events in human history.

The Fourth Kingdom is the New Rome

Pax Romana, it was called--Roman peace. For almost 1,000 years, Rome and its battle-hardened soldiers ruled much of the world. This was so during the days that Jesus Christ walked this earth. It will be true once again when Jesus returns.

The Roman Empire extended from Italy, Germany,

Scandinavia, and England in Europe, to Greece, Turkey, Persia, Israel, and Egypt. The Roman legions also were the conquerors and occupiers of Babylon, a fact that should stand out in our minds.

Bible prophecy tells us that in the last days there will be a revival of the Roman Empire. Again one man will control this vast stretch of valuable real estate. The prophet Daniel was given a picture of the dread nation-state system that would arise on the planet in the last days and go forth to conquer:

> After this I saw in the night visions, and behold a fourth beast, dreadful and terrible, and strong exceedingly; and it had great iron teeth: It devoured and broke in pieces, and stamped the residue with the feet of it: and it was diverse from all the beasts that were before it; and it had ten horns (Daniel 7:7).

This "Fourth Kingdom" that Daniel saw in his night visions will have a leader. He is described as a *little horn:* "I considered the horns, and, behold, there came up among them another little horn, before whom there were three of the first horns plucked up by the roots: and behold, in this horn were eyes like the eyes of man, and a mouth speaking great things" (Daniel 7:8).

Observe that this Fourth Kingdom has ten horns; that is, it is made up of ten nations or countries, and from among them comes up yet another *little horn*. But this little horn is not a country. Instead it has the "eyes of man and a mouth speaking great things." This is a picture of the dreaded Antichrist, also called the *beast* of Revelation 13.

The apostle John also had a vision from God in which he likewise saw this beast. The beast similarly had ten horns, which were described in Revelation 17:12 as representing *ten kings* who will rule with the beast. In the next verse (Revelation 17:13), we see that "these have one mind, and shall give their power and strength unto the beast."

Then, significantly, we read that the great religious and political system which will be set up by these ten kings (today we might call them presidents, prime ministers, chancellors, premiers, secretary-generals, etc.) will emanate--that is, have its source from--Babylon, "that great city, which reigneth over the kings of the earth" (Revelation 17:18).

Moreover, we find in the 17th chapter of Revelation that at the very time John was given this prophecy, this Mystery Babylon empire had a king who was in John's day then in power (see Revelation 17:10), but the *final* ruler of this great universal empire, John was told, "has not yet come; and when he cometh, he must continue a short space." So we are still today awaiting this final, last days world leader.

It should be noted that this great ruler, though he may dominate and subdue most of the earth, will not escape the judgment of God. In the very next verse (verse 11) we see that this beast "goeth into perdition." Just as Judas was the Son of Perdition, this man, too, will be the Son of Perdition (see II Thessalonians 2), and his final destination is the fires of everlasting hell.

When we view the incredible world drama occurring today, with earth-shattering events going on in Germany, Europe, the Soviet Union, the United States, China, and the Middle East, we come to this striking conclusion: the era in which the Bible prophesies that this final evil empire will arise to be led by the occultic Son of Perdition is *here, now.*

Germany's Four Reichs and Bible Prophecy

As we see the two Germanys merging and becoming one, our minds veer back to almost a half century ago, when this same united Germany marched across much of

Europe and Africa with its storm troopers and its terrible armed weaponry, slaughtering and savaging multitudes as it went. It is important to realize that Bible prophecy gives us many of the keys to today's world events. For example, we see in Ezekiel 38:6 that there is a nation, or a territory, called *Gomer* which, in the last days, will ally itself militarily with Russia (called the land of Gog, Meshech, and Tubal in *Ezekiel*), as well as Iran and Iraq (identified as Persia in *Ezekiel*), and Ethiopia, Libya, and Turkey/ Syria (identified as Togarmah in the Bible).

Historians tell us that *Gomer* is *Germany*. Evidently then, we will soon be presented with a spectacle in which both the Soviet Union and a strong united Germany take matters into their own hands by invading Israel and the Middle East with a combined military task force. Their objective no doubt will be to take the oil-rich lands of that region. This, they will reason, will put The Order in total control of the world's economies, since it is in the Middle East that is found the bulk of the earth's precious oil reserves.

The First Reich of Otto the Great

It is fitting that historic Gomer, or Germany, play this prophetic role. Adolf Hitler proclaimed that his was the Third Reich (imperial regime) of the revived Holy Roman Empire. The First Reich is regarded as that led by Germany's Otto the Great. He and the Catholic pope ruled the Holy Roman Empire in a spiritual and temporal sense in the tenth century A.D. The *New Rome* now being set up will also have both a political *and* religious leadership: church and state will be in one accord.

The Second Reich of Bismarck

Then there was the Second Reich, from 1871 to 1917. Otto Von Bismarck, greatly admired in today's Germany as a supreme warrior and leader, was the dictator of Germany during this period. It was Bismarck whose German infantry conquered France in 1871. With this great victory, Kaiser Wilhelm I of Prussia was crowned the first Kaiser. This should startle us when we realize that the word *Kaiser* literally means *Caesar!*

Emperor Wilhelm II, Wilhelm I's successor, you will recall, is the man who plunged the world into World War I. Like Hitler after him, he was a Jew-hater; once being quoted as saying, "A Jew cannot be a true patriot. He is something different, like a bad insect. He must be kept apart, out of a place where he can do mischief--even by pogroms if necessary."[11]

The first World War of Kaiser Wilhelm II was hideous in its bloodshed and ruination. This was the war where tanks were first used and in which tens of thousands suffered casualties as a result of heinous chemical warfare.

The Third Reich of the Nazis

Then along came Adolf Hitler, an occultic follower of Satan who established the Third Reich. Hitler claimed it would last for a thousand years or longer. Not true; it lasted a mere twelve. But during that short era, Hitler made his mark on the whole world. His sins and his transgressions may not be remembered by today's youth, but they should be.

What is shocking is that Adolf Hitler came to power in a *democratic* nation through the *popular vote* of the people. Today, there are those who are working hard to bring into being a One World Democratic Order. They say that such a political and economic Order will ensure freedom, justice, and sharing for all. Their contention is that a One World Democratic Order will guarantee against a mad dictator like Hitler ever again holding the reigns to such terrible power.

The truth, however, is that it is *not* a democratic framework of government that restrains men from committing atrocities and abominations; left to their own devices, without the loving nature of God within that comes from a born again experience (John 3:3), man will do evil no matter what the form of government. Hitler was astonishing proof of this very fact.

A Supernatural Rumbling in the Earth

Today there is a supernatural rumbling in the earth and it comes first from the direction of Europe, where the Fourth Reich is rising from the ashes of a war torn, post-war Europe. We may therefore well ask, has the ghost of Adolf Hitler been resurrected? Bible prophecy indicates the answer is *yes*. The ascension of a new Germany--united, powerful, determined, and assertive--will result in a *Fourth Reich.* A supreme World Leader is sure to follow.

Interestingly, there is still another astonishing event taking place that is highly significant as an indicator of Bible prophecy being fulfilled. I refer to the incredible restoration of ancient Babylon, the great city where Satan's hideous worldwide religion first began. As we will see in the following chapter, Babylon and Germany alike are destined to play key roles in the momentous days just ahead.

THIRTEEN

Babylon Comes Alive!
Lighting Up the Fiery
Furnaces Once Again

And upon her forehead was a name written,
MYSTERY, BABYLON THE GREAT, THE
MOTHER OF HARLOTS AND ABOMINATIONS
OF THE EARTH.

(Revelation 17:5)

The air was indeed filled with the burning of incense.
The music was so mythological in nature that you
could actually feel there was an evil presence in the
air... I heard them say that Ishtar (the goddess) is
returned again to Baghdad, the capital of Iraq. They
actually had a figure of the goddess Ishtar in the
ceremony as they worshipped. The entire ceremony
was New Age and occultic, filled with Babylonian
pagantry and attire.

Joseph Chambers
Babylon is Rising

Modern-day Iraq shocked the whole world
in the summer of 1990 by invading tiny,
oil-rich Kuwait, its next door neighbor in
the Persian Gulf. Thus began the strange spectacle of the
world standing by in dread and awe as the United States
of America, allied with other forces and with the moral

support of the United Nations, began to send in tens of thousands of military troops to counter the huge armies that Iraq dictator, Saddam Hussein, had put together over the previous decades.

Almost to a person, veteran political and military commentators were caught by surprise when Hussein's forces invaded Kuwait and threatened to take over Saudi Arabia as well as possibly other nations in the Middle East. At the time I began work on this book, conflict had not yet broken out in the Persian Gulf and peace seemed to be breaking out all over. Yet, I well knew that the dogs of war would soon awaken, fiercely violent after their brief nap. Bible prophecy must be fulfilled.

Another man who was not surprised was my good friend Joseph Chambers, pastor of a wonderful church in Charlotte, North Carolina, and editor of a fascinating prophetic newspaper, *End Times and Victorious Living*. In May, 1990 Dr. Chambers' lead article in his newspaper was entitled "Babylon Rises Again." I believe that the prophetic information reported in this article--an article written *before* Iraq and its dictator Hussein astonished the world and made headlines with their military invasion-- should be looked at once again.

The article declared that Babylon the Great was on the rise. And that the secret of its future could be found only by reference to Bible prophecy and especially the books of Revelation and Isaiah. Dr. Chambers observed that "The rebuilding of Babylon has caught the church leaders of our day by surprise and the ones I know are still denying that there is any significance. Very soon there will be no doubt."[1]

Words Of Prophecy Fulfilled

Again, I want to emphasize that these words were written and published *before* the Iraqi invasion of Kuwait, and their conclusions are based on the author's knowledge of the strength of Bible prophecy. Now let's examine another spectacular comment that Dr. Chambers made in that same article. He told his readers "Here are some things you can watch for that will help strengthen this powerful Biblical Truth:"

* Iraq will be increasingly in the world news.
* This small nation will become a sore spot in the Middle East and will gain political dominance.
* The rhetoric between Iraq and Israel will intensify.
* Watch for a peace initiative between Iraqi leaders and Israeli moderates. This will eventually lead to a covenant of peace.
* Don't put a timetable on what is happening. Leaders could well come and go before the ultimate events in this nation of destiny.[2]

The Revival of Mystery Babylon--and the New Rome

Not too long ago I had the opportunity to meet with Joseph Chambers, and we turned our attention to the momentous events breaking forth in Iraq and elsewhere in the Middle East. We noted that Babylon is geographically today's Iraq. Joseph and I recalled the prophecy in Zechariah 5:11 about the two angels who, in the last days, return the Mystery Woman--weighted down in all her wickedness--to Babylon. This prophecy is now being fulfilled. Dictator Hussein calls himself "the light of this world" and promotes the ancient Babylonian mysteries, and it is startling that he has chosen to restore the ruins of Babylon to their former glory. This is a great, ominous forewarning of horrible things to come.

If you will remember, Babylon and Sumeria were part and parcel of the Roman Empire of the Caesars. Therefore, the newly revived Holy Roman Empire, being formed today out of the United States of Europe, will consist not only of the numerous nations of Europe, especially the unified Germany, Italy, Belgium, England, etc., but will also take in many of the nations of the Middle East, including Babylon (Iraq), Turkey, Syria, Lebanon, and others. All of these nations were once under the heel of the legions of the vast Roman Empire.

In a booklet, *Babylon Rises Again*, that he is now developing into a full-length book, Dr. Joseph Chambers emphasizes the study of Revelation, Daniel, and other books of the Bible. These prophesy that the literal city of Babylon will be rebuilt in the last days and will then be destroyed a final time, never to be heard from again.

In a fascinating guidebook published by the Iraqi government, *From Nebuchadnezzar to Saddam Hussein: Babylon Rises Again,* the Iraqi mania to restore Babylon to world dominance once again is made evident. Just look at the opening statement from this book:

> In a glorious time, she is a lady of reviving centuries, rising dignified and holy, showing the great history of Iraq.
> Added to its magnificence and emphasizing its originality, the Phoenix of the new time rising alive from the ashes of the past, the face of bright present that places it on a golden throne and bringing back to it its charming youth and unique glory....

> Babylon survived the ages, defied all times, and overcame... It won the battle by virtue of its great heritage and the formidable men who carried that heritage... That produced unique heroes... so history can start with us so that it remains accomplished throughout the ages... Saddam Hussein who merges from Mesopotamia as the Hammurabi and as a Nebuchadnezzar. He has emerged at a time to shake the centuries old dust off its face.

Pageantry and Evil Reborn in Babylon

To fully gain perspective on this mind-boggling restoration of Babylon, it would be instructive for us to take a look at how Joseph Chambers described a massive celebration held in that city two years ago to commemorate the rebuilding of Babylon, now underway as a major construction project. Here is Dr. Chambers' eye witness description; he was there at the invitation of the Iraqi government and saw what can only be described as a ghost-like resurrection of the most wicked civilization that ever existed:

The mystic-sounding event begins. Background music with a mythological ring hails the drama of a returning monarch. King Nebuchadnezzar enters with great fanfare. Paganistic incense stills the air as the worshippers of this god-like king march to his tune. The ceremonial dress is the ancient Babylonian attire. Other than the amplification, strobe lights, and fireworks, it is very authentic. The air is poignant with excitement (or evil, depending on your perspective).

Clearly, Saddam Hussein is believed by the Iraqis to be the new Arabic Messiah ready to lead the Arab people to unparalleled greatness. The riches of this nation, with the world's second largest production of oil, has the wealth and the means to effect the entire world's economy. Will they be part of the Antichrist world government and help produce unparalleled prosperity for a short period? I have no doubt they will.[3]

Dr. Chambers continues his description of the gala event:

The air was indeed filled with the burning of incense. The music was so mythological in nature that you could actually feel there was an evil presence in the air...I heard them say that Ishtar (the goddess) is returned again

to Baghdad, the capital of Iraq. They actually had a figure
of the goddess Ishtar in the ceremony as they worshipped.
The entire ceremony was New Age and occultic, filled with
Babylonian pageantry and attire. It was breathtaking and
beautiful in a way... The devil can present moving and
stirring ceremonies, and from the study of the New Age
movement and the music, we know that people can be
possessed literally by demons when listening to New Age
mystical music.

Babylon the Great is at the very epicenter of Bible
prophecy. This is the place where goddess worship began
and was most prominent. Later, the worship of the goddess
spread throughout the known world. It is prophesied to
return to world prominence in the last days (Revelation
17). The authoritative book, *New Age Lies to Women*, by
my wife Wanda Marrs, chronicles the amazing resurgence
of the goddess in the 1990s not only in the New Age
Movement but even among some "Christian" congregations.

The Berlin-Babylon-Rome Connection: Will The Furnaces be Reignited?

The Bible establishes that in the last days, Babylon will
come back to life and there will be a Berlin-Babylon-
Rome connection. Hitler and his Jew-hating colleagues
established concentration camps in which they installed
ovens to incinerate the bodies of their Jewish victims. But
the Germans were not the first to commit such heinous
crimes. We read in Jeremiah and Daniel that because of
their transgressions the Lord gave the Israel nation into
captivity in Babylon. And not only that, but it is recorded
in Jeremiah 29:22, "that the Lord make thee like
Zedekiah and like Ahab, whom the King of Babylon
roasted in the fires."
Amazingly then, Hitler was not the first demonic-led

monster whose hateful and evil nature consumed the Jews in fiery furnaces. Today, Babylon's Saddam Hussein likewise has made threatening overtures against the Israelis. Indeed he longs to wipe them off the face of the map and give their lands back to the Arabs. Whether he will in fact be the leader of Iraq and the new Babylon at the time of the final shaking of the Middle East and of the days leading to Armageddon (See Joel 3:16) we cannot say for sure. But certainly the actions of Hussein give us cause to reflect on what prophecy tells us about the amazing events that are now occurring in the Middle East as well as in Germany and Europe.

Is The Order Behind the Resurgence of Babylon?

Something very evil has been loosed in the Middle East, and the financial cartel may be behind a good part of it. While Saddam Hussein spent most of the 1980s pressing a bloody war against his neighbor Iran, benefactors in the West opened their money bags and their armories pouring out gifts to the dictator. France alone supplied an estimated $12 billion worth of military hardware between 1981 and 1988. Iraq was also able to buy sophisticated technology for its missile development program from firms in Britain, Italy, Germany, and the United States. To finance his war, develop hideous new chemical weapons, and build up a huge war machine, Saddam needed a friendly banker, and he found the international banking conspiracy more than glad to bankroll him.[4]

Thus, both the aggression of Iraq and its rebuilding of Babylon were made possible by Western financial interests. This can best be understood in light of the fact there are definite, evil connections between Germany and Iraq, Berlin and Babylon. The rise of Babylon signals the emergence of the New World Order.

The Gate of Ishtar Brought To Berlin

During World War I, something quite remarkable happened. Even as the military forces of aggressor Germany were engaged in the trenches against those of France, Britain, and the United States, Kaiser Wilhelm II of Germany sent a military task force and a team of archaeologists down to Babylon. Their mission was to seize the stones and mosaic tiles that make up the ruined walls of the Gate of Ishtar, the great entrance to the city of ancient Babylon. Successful in this undertaking, Germany's soldiers brought the ruins back to Berlin where archaeologists reconstructed this tremendous monument. There today it sits in the Pergammon Museum.

Why has the Ishtar gate been restored? Why is it now in a museum in Berlin? The answer is that the fabulous Gate of Ishtar is symbolic of the revival of the Roman Empire, an expansive empire which ruled from Europe to the Middle East and encompassed Berlin, Rome, and Babylon in the days of Caesar. Germany was signaling its intent to revive ancient Rome!

No doubt, Kaiser Wilhelm (the word *Kaiser* means "Caesar," or emperor, in the German language) was led by occultic forces. He knew what he was doing. The Gate of Ishtar represents the glory of Babylon as the gateway to world power. Emblazoned on the Ishtar gate are, on the left, the great bull god, the father deity of the Babylonians; and on the right, the dragon. The horns of the bull have for centuries symbolized the devil. And, of course, the book of Revelation pictures the devil as that old dragon and serpent.

Kaiser Wilhelm obviously believed that Germany would gain great occultic powers by having the Gate of Ishtar standing once again in Berlin. He believed that Berlin would be the capitol of the new, revived Holy Roman Empire. This is why the Ishtar gate continues to be on display in Berlin: Germany is the western leg of the astonishing statue pictured in the book of Daniel--the two legged beast. Germany is to share with the restored Babylon of Iraq the newfound glory of olden times.

The Aryan Super-Race--Did it Come From Babylon?

Babylon shares with Germany a number of other curious characteristics as well. The lion was one of the great imperial symbols of Babylon and was adopted as such for Rome by the Roman Caesars. Not surprisingly, Adolf Hitler and his henchmen often conducted occultic ceremonies for the dreaded Gestapo at night with statues of mighty lions prominent on the stage, along with candles and other occultic, symbolic paraphernalia.

I have already noted that each nation, Germany and Babylon, used fiery furnaces to dispose of Jews. Yet another curious connection is the notion of the Aryan super race. Hitler believed that the Aryan race came from the area of Babylon and India (ruled by Babylon) and migrated from there into present-day Germany. He believed that this great Aryan white race was destined to become the Aquarian race of supermen and human deities.

I recently purchased a book from a neo-Nazi group entitled *The Endo-Sumerian Seals Deciphered*, written by a well-known and respected London anthropologist of his day named L. A. Waddell and published in 1925. This book maintains that there was an Aryan race, and that it originally came from Sumeria and Babylon.

Moreover, in her book, *The Initiation of The World*, New Age authority Vera Stanley Alder contends that "The vanguard of the Aryan race finally descended from the Gobi desert into India, having come from ancient Atlantis." According to Alder, the Aryans worshiped the god Agni, known to the Hindus as the fire god. It was to protect and preserve the pure Aryan blood, she writes, that the Hindu god Krishna developed the concept of caste systems. Thus, the lower caste in India, being brown, yellow, and colored, were not allowed to intermarry and mix with higher caste Aryans, who were white. From India the Aryan race is said to have moved on into Phoenicia, Greece, Rome, Germany, and into Britain.[5]

The late Joseph Campbell, author of a number of books on the mythologies, and a man who became a hero to millions of New Agers and others after being showcased by his good friend Bill Moyers (a CFR member) on a Public Broadcasting System (PBS) television series, affirmed much of what Alder has written. Campbell, who was known to despise Jews and held anti-Semitic views, suggested that the literature of what he called Aryan Greece and Rome is "alive with spiritual meaning."[6]

How interesting that those in today's neo-Nazi movements, as well as mythologists and New Agers like Joseph Campbell, in one way or another all support the poisonous racial views of Adolf Hitler. Hitler's conception of the Aryan race is still alive today. It is this Aryan race doctrine that spiritually unites modern-day Babylon with Berlin. In coming years we will see the hideous significance of the Berlin-Babylon connection and we will also discover a growing relationship between the Vatican, as the representative of a new united world faith, and these two capitols of the revived and restored Roman Empire. The Beast that was wounded (Rev. 13:3) is now rapidly being healed.

PART FOUR

Earth Days and Devil Nights

FOURTEEN

A Supernatural Faith for the New Millennium

How art thou fallen from heaven, O Lucifer... For thou has said in thine heart, I will ascend into heaven. I will exalt my throne above the stars of God... I will be like the Most High.

(Isaiah 14:12-15)

It has been thought that the sheep went to heaven and the goats went to hell. It is the other way around... The goats go to heaven...

Djwhal Khul, The Tibetan Master
The Rays and the Initiations

An acorn planted in the ground, if watered, nurtured and tended, someday becomes a majestic creation: a mighty oak tree offering shade, protection and beauty. Likewise, the seeds of evil, once planted in fertile soil and tended with destructive but powerful fervor, grow into awesome creations: huge, hideous, gnarled monstrosities with rotten, mired roots that are hidden from view, and poisonous fruit that clings seductively to twisted branches.

The evil that evolved into, first, the Mystery Babylon Religion and now, The Order, with its plans for world domination, did not spring forth into fullness all at once as the towering and monstrous creation it is today. Instead, its seed was initially planted millennia ago in the Garden of Eden when Lucifer told Eve the greatest of lies: Eat the forbidden fruit and "ye shall be as gods." Since that fateful hour, Satan has continuously worked his treachery and deception, culminating today in the insidious ravages of New Age occultism and the last days scheme of The Order.

The poisonous fruit from Satan's New Age tree are of many shapes, colors, and sizes, and their deadly toxins vary in viscosity and potency. The Plan of Alice Bailey's Tibetan Master, Djwhal Khul, has taken hold of the foul imaginations of The Order. The New Age is the chosen, occultic religion of the men who would rule the world. This is a driven group. Now they work incessantly, pushing The Plan, seducing men and women, and indoctrinating a steadily growing corps of supporters in every field of human endeavor. Tens of millions now profess New Age beliefs and many are proselytizing others. Evangelism is a popular preoccupation of New Age believers.

The Corrupt Objective of the New Age Deceivers

Why is Satan raising up this vast army of New Age spiritual leaders, teachers, and disciples and seeding them in all areas of human effort? Simply stated, his Plan is to remove from this planet every iota of Godly influence. His is a battle for the minds of men, women, and children, who are the pawns in his vile plan, the disposable raw material of conflict as Satan wars against God.

The primary goal, or objective, of Satan is a New Age Kingdom on Planet Earth. At the helm of this Kingdom will be Satan's "man," his Antichrist puppet (Revelation 13). This dark Kingdom will be the revival of the Mystery Babylon religion in which the Mother Goddess was adored and worshiped (Revelation 17). Thus, New Age teacher and writer Joshua Halpern assures his readers that:

Soon, very soon, there will be millions of us who are ready to acknowledge our common roots.... The day is fast approaching when all of humanity will realize they originate within the Rainbow Mother. By celebrating the return of the Goddess we help usher in the Light of Truth.[1]

Halpern also rouses his New Age followers to get ready to take action:

You must join your families into great circles of families. You must get organized and prepare yourselves for the changes that are coming. By the year 2000 the whole planet must be free. All the nations must come into the circle.... Mothers and fathers with children by their side will look in the same direction.... You are the Children of the Dawn.[2]

New Age authorities proclaim that the Piscean Age, the Age of Jesus Christ, is ending, and a glorious new Aquarian Age is dawning. The Christians have reigned for 2000 years, they say; now it's *our* turn. The Christian Age is said to be the dark, black ages while the coming New Age is an era of light: Vera Stanley Alder, for example, writes of the "Black Age" of outward ignorance which "has lasted two thousand years."[3] Now, trumpets Alder, all that is over. Now comes the "Golden Age."[4]

Kai King, publisher of *Gabriel's Horn*, a prominent New Age magazine, also writes of the New Age ruled over by God the Mother:

Now as we pass from the Piscean Age ... we find ourselves in a time when we must express love ... and the Great

Oneness... is pouring down... for those who are
experienced and live in the Aquarian Age. The New Age.
The age of the extreme influence from God the Mother.[5]

Alice Bailey's demon spirit guide, Djwhal Khul, the
Tibetan Master, related to her that the New Age is not
only the end of the age of Jesus Christ, it is to be a time
when heaven shall come to earth. However, he said, Jesus
was wrong about the dividing of the sheep and the goats:

> It has been thought that the sheep went to heaven and the
> goats went to hell. It is the other way around. The goat in
> Capricorn is the initiate and from a certain esoteric angle
> the goats do go to heaven because they function in the
> spiritual kingdom.... The sheep remain on earth... until
> they become goats...[6]

"Entrance into heaven," declares Djwhal Khul, "is entrance into the Aquarian Age... and Piscean (Christian)
forces will be receding rapidly." Ruth Montgomery, the
psychic known as the Herald of the New Age and author
of the bestselling biography of astrologer Jeanne Dixon,
concurs. "The earth and her solar system are signaling the
end of a grand cycle of the ages," she writes in her book
Aliens Among Us?[7] During this New Age epoch--the New
Age--says Montgomery, *only humans who are suitable* will
become as gods. You must possess the higher vibrations
of the New Age to survive, she explains. For instance, you
must be willing to admit that *"You* are I AM, the eternal."[8]

Montgomery fails to mention, however, that it is
blasphemy to proclaim oneself the great I AM, the eternal. This is the name of the most High God, our Lord and
Savior, Prince of Peace, and Avenger of His people. It is
His name and His alone.

It is the intermediate goal of the New Age to cause
people to rebel against the true God of the Bible and to
believe that they are deities. Once Satan has the person in
this heretical frame of mind, then the battle is won. The

individual will then be called for greater service to the Prince of Darkness. And with a mind clouded and confused, he or she will comply. The individual will have become a member, knowingly or unknowingly, of the Satanic conspiracy.

Exposing Satan's Divine Plan

The Order's decades-long drive to induce men to believe in the New Age religion has been supremely successful. This conspiracy has grown so huge that on December 31, 1988, it is estimated that 875 million New Age believers around the globe participated in the colossal event called World Healing Day. Master-minded by the Planetary Commission, an international New Age networking group headquartered in Austin and headed by John Randolph Price, at 12:00 noon Greenwich Mean Time these millions of New Agers visualized and meditated simultaneously, seeking to bring in the New Age Kingdom.

The huge turnout for World Healing Day was not a surprise. Price had told his followers and the leaders of hundreds of other participating New Age organizations that if these millions joined their mind powers collectively in a Global Mind-Link, the world could not only be catapulted into the gloriously radiant and dazzling New Age, but that each participant might well become *as a god!*

However, while godhood was the carrot, Price also held out a stick. According to Price's spirit guide (demon), Asher, if the event did not succeed, the spiritual hierarchy in the unseen world would be forced to use more drastic measures to bring in the New Age paradise. Nature will then enter her "cleansing cycle," warned Asher, and more than two billion people must be destroyed--wiped off the face of the earth.

This is all part of the "Divine Plan," Asher has

confided to Price, a New Age Plan for the salvation of the world.[9] Driven by his demonic guide, John Randolph Price has become one of the greatest proselytizers of The Plan in the world today. Price's principal contribution to Satan's Secret Plan is his founding of the Planetary Commission. Jesus Christ gave His followers the Great Commission, commanding them to go forth and preach the gospel to all nations. Today, Satan has his New Age counterfeit, the Planetary Commission, with its mandate for New Age believers to spring into action and smother peoples everywhere with the false gospel capsulized by The Plan.

In his book, *The Planetary Commission*, John Randolph Price strives to inspire all New Age believers to get in step with The Plan:

> For you to be an effective member of the Planetary
> Commission, you should understand your role in . . . the
> Divine Plan. . . . Yes, the salvation of the world does
> depend on you. . . . The *Divine Plan* is the strategy and the
> blueprint for each individual man and woman, for the
> entire human race, and for the planet self . . .[10]

Sadly, John Randolph Price and the tens of millions of other New Agers now working feverishly to pollute our minds are simply fulfilling Lucifer's despicable Plan, a plan of evil that in its visionary form has been in existence for millennia. The prophet Isaiah, over 2000 years ago, unmasked Lucifer's grandiose scheme to bring his Plan to pass--and Isaiah announced what shall be the ultimate end of the Evil One's corrupt imaginings:

> How art thou fallen from heaven, O Lucifer, son of the
> morning! how art thou cut down to the ground, which didst
> weaken the nations! For thou has said in thine heart, I will
> ascend into heaven. I will exalt my throne above the stars
> of God: I will sit also upon the mount of the congregation,
> in the sides of the north: I will ascend above the heights of

the clouds; I will be like the most High. Yet thou shalt be brought down to hell, to the sides of the pit (Isaiah 14:12-15).

While today we are now being taught the lie that positive thinking will bring internal happiness, abundant health and material success, truly it can be said that *Satan is the World's Greatest Positive Thinker.* In Isaiah (above), we discover that the devil made five consecutive, positive affirmations (or "positive confessions"). Yet, neither the demented powers resident in the awesome mind of Satan nor the mind power of mere mortals shall prevail over God's will.

New Age Principles Taught

What has John Randolph Price's shadowy master Asher revealed to him about the new spiritual principles to be taught in the New Age? Price's bestselling book, *The Planetary Commission*, contains several corrupt but revealing guidelines and rules. First, individuals are to "fully awaken" to the divinity within them so they can function more completely as "illumined ones."[11] Psychic powers, such as the reading of auras around the bodies, are to be encouraged.

People are also to be taught "our kinship with all life--all nature--the rocks, plants, animals." In other words, that all is God, that God is an energy force, and not a person.[12]

Another New Age principle to be taught is that of group, or collective salvation. God did not die on the cross for your sins, people will be told. New Age doctrine teaches that the "idea" of individual salvation, as taught by traditional Christianity, went out with the ending of the astrological Age of Pisces, the age of Jesus. In the New Age, the era in which man is himself Christ and God, personal salvation is not as important as group and planetary consciousness.

"The time of spiritual growth through spiritual isolation is gone," Price states. "It went out with the Age of Pisces. In the Aquarian Age, the Age of Spirituality, the emphasis is on . . . the group."[13]

Price's spirit guide also has given him a spiritual teaching to help people, young and old, identify the Antichrist. The Antichrist, according to the New Age teaching, is not Satan's man of sin, who comes to take the reigns of government into the last days. Asked, "How do you define the Antichrist," Price provides this chilling definition:

> Any individual or group who denies the divinity of man . . .
> The illumined ones have identified this inner adversary as Satan or Lucifer.[14]

This sick New Age definition is no doubt resulting in many people disbelieving the Bible's clear teachings. At the same time, it causes the world to view Christians as the Antichrist, because no Bible-believing Christian believes in the "divinity of man." There is only one God and one name in heaven and earth identified as divine: Jesus Christ (see Philippians 2:9-11).

Serve the Plan . . . At Any Cost!

The total devotion New Age leaders pay to The Plan explains why their leaders have been so successful in their untiring offensive. Alice Bailey, one of the most influential New Age leaders of this century, calls for "absorbing devotion to The Plan." She has said that New Age disciples worldwide must serve The Plan "at any cost."[15]

Bailey also gives us revealing information on who is

behind the New Age Plan. She states that shortly a great occultic "World Savior" will burst upon the world scene.[16] He will come, she maintains, to bring "Light and Love and Power and Death."[17]

> Then shall the Coming One appear, His footsteps hastened through the valley of the shadow by the One of awful power . . .[18]

Bailey makes clear this "Coming One" will not be Jesus, but a greater one whom she describes as "Sanat," also known as the One Initiator the Lord of the World. We can be quite sure that "Sanat" is simply a scrambling of the word "Satan."

Another top New Age leader, Benjamin Creme, says that The Plan calls for momentous changes in families and that new guidelines for children and young people are definitely included. The nuclear family of parents and children must give way to the concept of Global Family, Creme insists, and the education system must take this into account. According to Creme's teaching of the New Age Plan, the children being born in this generation are to possess magical ESP powers their parents do not, such as mental telepathy, the ability to read other people's minds.[19] Creme further states that the New Age "Christ," Lord Maitreya, has told him to relay this important message to the world:

> My people are everywhere. Join them. Become one of them . . . take part in the Great Plan.[20]

> My Plan is to reveal My presence shortly on a much wider scale and to show men that the New Age is dawning. . . . Join My army, my friends and brothers, and cleanse this world of hate.[21]

The Alternative is Annihilation

Keep in mind that when this spirit who goes by the name "Lord Maitreya" speaks of cleaning the world of hate, what he really means is eradicating Christians off the face of the earth. Creme has boldly proclaimed that those who refuse to join the New Age faith will be forced to "withdraw from this life." Asked by a questioner exactly what this phrase meant, Creme bluntly answered, "the alternative is annihilation."[22]

Lord Maitreya, Creme's version of the New Age "Christ," will, at his coming, Creme says, cause everyone on earth to *love* and *serve* The Plan. Maitreya is said to be the "Master of the Masters, the Teacher alike of angels and of men." As the servant and agent of another, much greater Lord whom Creme identifies as "Sanat," Maitreya "comes as a World Teacher to inaugurate the age of Aquarius."[23] Maitreya is said to have only one motive: "It is to serve The Plan:"

> My Plan is that the world should be changed by man. The Law forbids all else. Therefore, my friends, I depend on you to execute my Plan, and thus prepare for the New World. . . . Taking stock of My Mission thus far, I see changes so radical that My Plans unfold sooner than I anticipated. This being so, my brothers, My face will become known to you before long.[24]

It is apparent that the New Age's Lord Maitreya is, in fact, a prototype of the Beast and Antichrist we are warned of in the Bible (Revelation 6 and 13). His thinly disguised master, Sanat, is, in reality, Satan. And it is thus Satan who has issued the New Age Plan to take captive the souls of our children.[25]

The New Age guardians and administrators of The Plan go to great pains to disguise and conceal their black-hearted campaign. Frequently, they cloak their efforts behind shadowy and vague terms, phrases, code words, and acronyms. Thus, we find New Age occultism masquerading behind multitudes of masks. Here are just a few such masks: human potential movement, self-love, self-actualization, self-realization, higher self, transformation therapy, sensitivity training, enlightenment, transcendental meditation, holistic thinking, holism, gnosis, the life force, UFO's, mysticism, spirit channeling, the perennial philosophy, community, globalism, unity, ESP, mind powers, inner potential, healing of the memories, spiritualism, the ancient wisdom, paradigm shift, the Third Wave, new thinking, possibility thinking, personal mythologies, white magic, Age of Aquarius, dream work, cosmic consciousness, higher consciousness, right brain/ left brain, metaphysics, Zen, crystal powers, self-empowerment, the New Spirituality, New Thought, The Force, Dianetics, centering, visualization, humanistic psychology, transpersonal psychology, pyramid powers, Kundalini power, polarity, God is Energy, Harmonic Convergence, planetization, King Arthur and Camelot, World Peace Movement, paganism, the High Religion, the Old Religion, the Gaia Hypothesis, Mother Earth, Yin/ Yang, Tao, Planetary Synthesis, Montessori, regression therapy, rebirthing, symbol therapy, the Mother Goddess, Samadhi, feminist spirituality, Age of Enlightenment, Golden Age, Christian Science, Religious Science, the New Pentecost, the Source, the Reality, the Presence.

Now all the phrases and terms are indicative that Satan has, in the New Age movement and religion, put together an incredible array of different groups, organizations, and personalities to execute his evil Plan. My book, *Texe Marrs Book of New Age Cults and Religions,* is a readable and authoritative reference guide to these many cults and groups. Their terms and codewords may vary, but all New Age teachers and leaders wholly agree on their basic doctrines.

Why, then, this bewildering and confusing hodge-podge of terms and phrases to describe New Age beliefs, practices and goals? Plain and simple, the reason is to obscure and protect the overall Plan.

The Plan to be Secret and Occultly Guarded

The overall Plan of the New Age to usher in a Luciferian One World System as well as their blueprint to capture the souls of men and women is not easily discerned. It takes voluminous research and investigation to discover just where all the tentacles of the Beast lead. In addition, from my own experience as a Christian investigator and researcher, I know that only the Holy Spirit of God can lead a person to an understanding of The Plan. The Bible teaches us regarding the last days conspiracy of Satan that "none of the wicked shall understand, but the wise shall understand" (Daniel 12:10).

The New Age masters do not even let many of their top insiders know *all* The Plan. So most New Agers are unknowingly following a carefully laid out Plan, the true, hideous dimensions of which they are only vaguely--if at all--aware. They, too, are victims of the lie of the New Age and the plot of The Order. But they are victims by choice, having rejected the Truth (II Thessalonians 2.)

Djwhal Khul, David Spangler and other demon and human New Age leaders have admitted that the full dimensions of The Plan are a closely guarded secret not divulged to the masses. Khul says that the activities of the New Age elite in carrying out the Plan are "occultly guarded."[26] The word *occult* means hidden from view or concealed.

David Spangler, in his supposedly divinely inspired *Revelation: The Birth Of A New Age,* reveals that "gradually, silently," "behind the scenes," The Plan has been worked by human and spirit disciples.[27]

Praise our Lord Jesus Christ, He told us in His Word

that the elect would *not* be deceived (Matthew 24:24). This is, I am positive, why God has inspired me to write this book exposing The New Age Plan and its atrocious intent. What Satan desires to keep secret, so he can do his dirty work without hindrance, we Christians should shout from the housetops. The more people who know of this horrible, vicious Plan of Satan, the more victims we can rescue for God's Kingdom. God will not let His chosen perish in ignorance. Satan's cruel Plan shall be revealed.

The Demon Spirits in Charge of the Plan

There is no doubt whatsoever that every New Age and occult organization and group in existence today was founded at the inspiration of demonic spirits. The men of The Order, I am positive, are led by these demonic beings. For example, John Randolph Price's inspiration was a spirit who called himself "Quartus" as well as a demon calling himself "Asher." Alice Bailey and Robert Muller were initiated by "Djwhal Khul," and Elizabeth Claire Prophet has spoken of "Count St. Germain" and a number of other spirit entities who guide her influential New Age ministry.

Sometimes, the demonic spirits in charge of The Plan come pretending to be dead relatives and other loved ones. Sometimes, these familiar spirits (called an "abomination unto the Lord"--see Deuteronomy 18) go on to become lifelong companions of the New Age believer whom they possess. Often, these spirits encourage the person to sin and disobey God's will.

In her book *Companions In Spirit,* New Age spirit channeler Laeh Garfield, gives us a fascinating example of a demon spirit who comes to incite a person to commit unholy acts. Garfield, who teaches that New Agers should learn to communicate with and be guided by spirits, relates this account of her friend, Molly, supposedly visited by the demon spirit of her deceased mother:

My friend Molly was trying to broaden her tolerance for different lifestyles. She had been raised a Mennonite herself, and had turned out a strong, highly principled woman. But she had also grown up with a lot of narrow-mindedness and joyless disapproval. Although she was attempting to be more flexible with her own teenage sons, it was proving very difficult for her to ignore the rules of her upbringing now that her boys were bringing beer home, smoking marijuana on occasion, and inviting girls over to the house.

Molly didn't discuss her inner conflict directly. For quite some time the only clues were her nervous laughter and her frequent references to how strict her mother had been. Her mother had passed on several years prior to this.

One night just before bedtime Molly looked across the room and saw her mother standing there--with a cigarette in her hand. A shock went right through Molly's heart. "Oh," she whispered to herself, "that couldn't be Mother." But thereupon she heard her mother say, "Well, Molly, I've learned a few things since I died." With that, the figure disappeared.

In the months that followed, Molly saw no more of her mother. Evidently the one visit was enough. Molly felt certain that her mother had come in spirit to give her permission to loosen up a bit, and this was all she needed to begin viewing her own life and that of her boys with a kinder, less stringent perspective.[28]

Building of Networks

However, the demon spirits in charge of accomplishing Satan's Plan to destroy have greater work to do than to merely encourage--as they do--such sinful acts as marijuana smoking, beer drinking and smoking cigarettes. Their foulest work, promoting The Plan, is of cosmic significance and they are trained well for their mission. They work by building networks of New Age believers on earth.

Each of these coordinating and cooperating networks of individuals, groups, organizations, and churches, have their own part to play in The Plan. Some New Age networking organizations are active promoting guided imagery and visualization in schools, others are in charge of TV programming. They work to pervert our minds with shows which are brim full of sexual license, magic, sorcery, and Satanic violence and evil. There are also New Age networks guided by hidden spirit guides which have infiltrated the medical professions, and so forth.

The men and women at the heads of these actively working networks are the "nucleus"--the core group chosen by Satan as his front-line warriors. As Barry McWaters describes in *Conscious Evolution: Personal And Planetary Evolution*, it is this nucleus of hard-core New Age leaders that will be the catalyst for the New Age Kingdom to come into being. A quantum leap will then occur as "The Plan" is served:

> Significant numbers of individuals and groups are consciously working toward critical mass.... A part of humanity will form the nucleus. At some special moment, as individual cells begin to relate as one, a quantum leap will occur....

> Already there are a number of groups--World Servers for the New Age, Planet Stewards, Warriors of the Rainbow,

Children of the Dawn, etc.--that envision a unification.... The parts ... are being called together.... A network of light is forming.[29]

The Ascended Masters--Satan's well-oiled and cohesively trained cadre of demon spirits--are supervising the activities of this growing New Age "network of light."

The Masters ... are here with a particular mission.... Through the silent, hidden work of the Masters, men and women throughout the world are beginning to intuitively understand the Truth ... and it is only a matter of time before the dawning (of the New Age).[30]

The Hidden Threads of Conspiracy

Yes, there is a New Age conspiracy--a conspiracy in which those at the top, The Order, are personally led by Satan and his demons. Meanwhile, those at the bottom of the pyramid--the worker bees--toil in the New Age hive never even realizing who the royal one is who sits at the apex, giving the orders.

Moreover, Satan has shown his uncanny ability to bring the top leadership in the New Age together as necessary to cross-pollinate their evil schemes and designs on our kids. Jean Houston, a New Age psychologist noted for her theories of evolution and the pagan mythologies, tells the story that, as a young girl, she used to cross Central Park in New York City on her way to school. Often she would come upon an elderly, gray-haired gentleman in the park, sitting on a bench or walking around. The man told Jean to simply call him "Telly." She and "Telly" would sit and chat for long periods and she became entranced at his ideas and his manner.

Years later, when Houston studied philosophy in college, she saw a picture of Teilhard de Chardin, the heretical New Age author and exclaimed, "But this is my friend, Telly, the old gentleman in the park!"

Certainly, the early meeting as a child of Houston and Teilhard de Chardin was no accident. Satan no doubt intended for this evil individual, de Chardin, a Catholic priest who had rejected the Jesus of the Bible and instead had written that man is himself an evolving god, to meet and influence Jean Houston. His success is apparent by the fact that today, Houston is one of the principal architects of the New Age perversion of psychology, a teacher of evolution, and a prime promoter of The Plan.

The New Age Plan is a carefully devised instrument which is the result of much preparation and hard work by Satanic forces. For example, Foster Bailey states in the revealing *Running God's Plan*, that the "Hierarchy," which evidently functions for Satan much like a demonic Board of Directors, "holds a general conference twice in a century." At these conferences, says Bailey, "new hierarchical projects are proposed and changes in focus and emphasis are instituted."[31]

Bailey further states that at the last big conference of this behind-the-scenes hierarchy, three prime areas were targeted for exploitation: education, religion, and government. This accounts perhaps for not only the New Age drive for a One World Religion and One World Government but for Satan's all-out assault against the education system in the past few decades. The conquest of our classrooms is today almost complete.

Paul told us that in the last days, "things would wax worse and worse with men deceiving and being deceived" (II Timothy 3:13). This astonishing prophecy is being fulfilled. The first stages of the New Age Plan were implemented gradually at first, but now The Plan is progressing at a rapid pace. This is by design. The New Age leadership was to increasingly teach and bring in the tenets of The Plan so that the world would grow to believe that the Plan was *normal* and *natural* in man's evolutionary progress. In this way, advised Djwhal Khul, the Tibetan Master, "gradually the idea or concept of the Masters will be inculcated and steadily accepted." Emphasis on the unfolding "Plan would be steady until, finally, outright success will be achieved."[32]

Finally, Khul confides, when the "Christ" (*not* Jesus) is crowned king of the Planet:

> The time will come when the fact of the presence on earth of the (New Age) Christ as Head of the Hierarchy and Director of the Kingdom of God will be accepted; *men will also realize the truth of the present revolutionary statement that at no time has He ever left the earth.*[33]

The time of the appearance of the New Age Christ may be close at hand. But though virtually the whole world will be deceived by him, true Christians will easily discern this counterfeit is not the real Christ. All that's necessary is to read God's Word and His prophecies. They both reveal the coming of the real messiah and explain how to spot the imposter.

FIFTEEN

Possession is Nine-tenths of the Law

For if he that cometh preacheth another Jesus, *whom we have not preached, or if ye receive* another spirit, *which ye have not received, or* another gospel, *which ye have not accepted, ye might well bear with him.*
(II Corinthians 11:4)

You do well to remember your friends in the unseen. Companying with them the more you live in the Unseen World, the gentler will be your passing when it comes.

As told by "God" to the two
anonymous authors of *God Calling*

There is a well-known saying in common law that "possession is nine-tenths of the law." In the occult world, this old law applies with full force. Many of the men who mastermind the international conspiracy to bring in a One World Political/Economic Order and a New Age World Religion are under the foolish misconception that they are in control of their own destinies, that they are free agents.

In fact, he who Satan possesses he controls. In this chapter I will provide ample evidence that these men are controlled by demonic forces, and I will show how this control is exercised by demonic entities. Having willingly linked their futures with the Adversary, these evil men will someday suffer judgment at the hand of God for their consuming greed and their debauchery. The servant is not greater than the master and if Satan be judged, these men also--his accomplices--will go into perdition.

The hellish blueprint Satan has devised to spiritually and physically rip our nation apart and establish his Antichrist leader on the world throne is a reflection of the darkest side of Satan's monstrously evil personality. Satan strives--with great success--to keep the dark and terrible regions of his mind a veiled secret. Thus he almost always approaches us as an Angel of Light, as a hero or heroine, and as something good and positive, virtuous and desirable. Yet, because his mind is so infested with his vain and twisted thoughts and goals, neither Satan and his demons nor their human New Age followers can long conceal the depth of their twisted imaginations.

Satan is communicating his Secret Plan to his conspiratorial agents on earth by continually filling up their imagination with the seeds of The Plan which he desires them to nurture and bring into maturity. Few individuals caught up in the New Age religion, consumed with lust for money, or obsessed with the desire for power, truly understand the extent to which Satan controls and programs their minds as if they were puppets.

New Age disciples and their masters, the Lords of Money, are led to believe that they themselves are captains of their own fate and co-creators of their own life script. But in reality it is the manipulative Satan who punches the keys and pulls all the strings. They are his obedient, if unwitting, slaves. He is their master and they will obey. Without the unequalled power of God in his life, man is no match for a determined opponent like Satan. Thus, the masses willingly serve him while protesting they do not.

However, many in the *highest echelons* of occultism *do* know whom they serve. Through the New Age process called transformation or *kundalini* (also called rebirthing, initiation, self-empowerment, and other terms), they have been initiated by the dark forces in the hidden dimension and appraised of their role in The Plan. I believe that today there are tens of thousands who well understand that it is Satan who rules their lives and dictates their daily actions. And certainly the top people of the money elite are not unwitting servants of the devil.

144,000 Rainbow Warriors Chosen

Jose Arguelles, a one worldism advocate and college professor who coordinates a vast network of New Age organizations, has revealed that on August 17, 1987 during the worldwide Harmonic Convergence event, exactly 144,000 New Agers were culled out by the spiritual Hierarchy (i.e., demon powers) as "Rainbow Warriors." These 144,000, says Arguelles, know who they are and recognize their key role as the future leadership in the coming New Age World Order.[1]

Arguelles has said that this New World Order, the New Age kingdom of heaven on earth, will be fully ushered in by the year 2000. Even before that date, however, the New Age "Christ" will appear to take the reigns of world government. According to Arguelles, this may occur as early as 1992.

Arguelles says the chosen 144,000 are united in surrender to the "higher intelligence that rules this planet," obviously a veiled reference to Lucifer. Evidently, the lower level New Age followers are ignorant of the true identity of this higher intelligence.[2]

Benjamin Creme, advocate of the counterfeit "Christ," Lord Maitreya, explains that there are two major groups or divisions of New Age followers. The first group--"the inspired ones"--are consciously aware that they are receiving their instructions from their superiors in the Spirit World--the Masters as he calls them. The second group receives impressions only:

> The Masters now impress the minds of thousands of people who are quite unaware of this fact...

> These two divisions--both of them are receiving but one is consciously aware that it is coming from the Master and the other thinks "Ah ha"... I've had a great idea! "What I must do is this. I feel I must do this. I must. Yes." They don't realize it is from the Master--so they think it is their own idea.[3]

As Creme alludes, the vast majority of New Agers are unknowing, deceived victims, just as the vast majority of Germans were deceived by Hitler and his occult Third Reich. Thus we now view the spectacle in which thousands of teenagers dabble in the occult worship of satanic rock stars, believing this is harmless. Meanwhile, deluded adult men and women are gulled into joining various New Age and one world cults and groups. Alice Bailey's demon guide, Djwhal Khul, points out that the souls of these unwitting people are "occultly inspired" and driven to "unconscious cooperation with The Plan."[4]

A Behind-the-Scenes Activity

We see, then, that Satan is counting on the "unconscious cooperation" of the masses who are led to deny Christianity and to engage in the most heinous and terrible of occult practices, all the time proclaiming their innocence and right behavior. He needs these millions of people as pawns for his high stakes game of rebellion against Almighty God. Therefore, as Djwhal Khul admits, much of The Plan and the activities of the New Age elite are "occultly guarded."[5]

"This preparation for Aquarius is a tremendous operation," David Spangler agrees, which "has been birthed behind the scenes."[6]

Well, Spangler is wrong. The New Age cannot shield and keep hidden its "secret project" to harm families while seizing world power and dominion. I praise our Lord Jesus Christ that he has guided my path so I can rip asunder Satan's "occultly guarded" veil and expose his damaging activities.

Satan's Appeal to The Dark Side

In the Bible we find the remarkable and profound truth that Jesus Christ is the Light of this world. His Word is like a glowing bright lamp in the darkness. But once a person rejects this light, once the wick in God's lamp is extinguished in the life of an individual, the darkness rushes in to fill up the void. In the many New Age and occultic doctrines and practices, Satan serves us a veritable smorgasbord, or cornucopia, of dark spiritual offerings. Satan appeals to the dark side within every person who rejects Jesus Christ and His Light.

New Age sorceress and shaman Lyn Andrews, author of such mammoth bestselling books as *Crystal Woman* and *Jaguar Woman*, encourages her readers and fans to become acquainted with their dark sides. "Within the dark side is the secret, the seed of knowledge," she writes.[7] There, deep within and hidden, Andrews says, is the "primal energy," the dark side that is your power.

Satan gives his marching orders and instructions to his earthly disciples by dredging up and infilling this dark side within their own psyches, or souls. Robert Leichtman, M.D., and Carl Japikse, two prominent New Age authors and teachers, stress that New Age believers must work with "the living archetypal forces" (translated "demons" by knowledgeable Christians) so they can play their part on earth with greater effectiveness. These forces, say Leichtman and Japikse, have "the power to transform our thinking and behavior:"[8]

> To work with these divine forces, therefore, we must be prepared not just to interact with them, but to be changed by them . . . to be inspired by them to establish new priorities and values, based on what these living archetypal forces are striving to accomplish, not just what we want.[9]

We invite these forces, they explain, by using occult systems of divination, such as Tarot cards, the I Ching, numerology, the Runes, and astrology, and by reading science fiction and fantasy. These "archetypal forces," confide Leichtman and Japikse, may come to us as spirit entities from another realm or as mythological, ancient gods and goddesses (archetypes). In whatever form, image, or shape they come to us, say Leichtman and Japikse, we must respond to them and let them have their way. They are said to be "truly lights of heavens" from the divine mind of the Universe--The Force. Therefore, we obey their urgings and take prompt action to carry out their desires: "We can only harness a divine force when we are willing--and able--to serve as its inspired agent on earth."[10]

True Believers

The highest level cadre of Satan's human followers and conspirators are usually true believers who open themselves to evil after once and for all rejecting the truth found in God's Word. They are then assigned demon spirits who progressively lead them into the deeper initiations and occult perversions of the New Age. However, the people in the lower echelons of the conspiracy are not always as conscious of who is the real master behind the scenes.

First time experimenters and dabblers in the occult often operate at the outer perimeter of occultism. Little do they know that they are like ripe fruit waiting to be picked by Satan's end time harvesters. This is especially true of adults and kids alike who play around with crystals and ouija boards, get involved in fantasy games such as Dungeons & Dragons, and begin reading witchcraft and other occultic books.

It is at this early stage of involvement that Satan, justifiably feeling himself invited, moves in, sending lying demons to the individual whose ultimate goal is to recruit the young person or the adult into the worldwide networking system of the New Age.

Inheriting the Darkness

Most of the higher level members of The Order, the men who run the Trilateral Commission, the Council on Foreign Relations, the Priory of Sion, the Freemasonry Orders and so on, enter this world marked for later initiation into the mysteries of Satan's kingdom. Their fathers, and sometimes grandfathers before them, were members of the same secret societies and conspiratorial groups. Thus from birth, they are educated on their subsequent role in "the Great Work," the task of "illuminating the world." Still, if these men choose to renounce their unholy lifestyle and turn to Jesus Christ, God has the power to free them of this generational link with evil.

God Calling . . . Or Devil on the Line? Illuminating the Masses

While the elite among the conspirators safeguard the Master Plan and keep their subversive operations secret, they also work to inspire the masses to unwittingly join the conspiracy. One way to do this is to mass-produce demonically inspired books (often given to them by "automatic writing"). One such book is *God Calling*. The tale of how this book, produced by a disciple of Hitler's inner circle, came into such wide usage is a fascinating example of how Satan's forces--demonic and human--operate.[11]

Recently on a major Christian television show, I exposed the book *God Calling* as a fraud: a cleverly worded, smooth-as-silk counterfeit of the devil. Since that program, I have received overwhelming support from Christians who had this book in their home and knew *something* was wrong with it but couldn't figure out exactly what. As one woman remarked, "every time I began to read it, the Holy Spirit would send me warning signals. I became so agitated inside I had to put the book aside.

Incredibly, *God Calling* has been called a "Christian classic" because it has been sold in Christian bookstores for decades and has even hit the bestseller list. In fact, it is only one of a number of New Age and occult books--some of which have been around for years--which claim to have been written directly by God.

The Unholy New Age "Bibles"

If we accept *God Calling* as authentic, then should we not accept some or all of the other New Age and occult books and "Bibles" as legitimately authored directly by "God" or Jesus?"

Here is just a partial list of some of the books I have personally surveyed which purport to be authored by "God" or "Jesus":

The Book of Urantia
The Aquarian Gospel of Jesus Christ
Starseeds
The Jesus Letters
A Course in Miracles
A New Teaching for Humanity
The Law of One
The Keys of Enoch

Some of these fake "Bibles" are powerfully and persuasively written. The *Book of Urantia*, for example, is 2,097 pages long. Moreover, the combined sales of these books is in the millions.

Actually, *God Calling* is perhaps *the least credible* of all the many fakes now claiming to be inspired by "God" or "Jesus." Consider the fact that *God Calling* doesn't even divulge who its authors are other than identifying them as "two anonymous women" and you have a recipe for disaster. The anonymous authors, also called the "two listeners," claim to have been given the book directly by "Jesus." It was their claim, then, that this is God's Word, as equally authoritative as the Holy Bible.

However, as we shall see, Jesus did not author *God Calling*, nor were the many other New Age "Bibles" and "scriptures" received by divine inspiration.

We must remember that the Bible warns us of "another gospel" (Galatians 1:6-9) and "another Jesus" (II Corinthians 11:4). Jesus Himself alerted us that in the last days there would be many false "Christs" coming in His name (Matthew 24:5).

Unmasking Mr. A. J. Russell

Then, there's Mr. A. J. Russell, listed on the cover of *God
Calling* as "editor." Russell says in the introduction of *God
Calling* that the two anonymous women authors came to
him in the 1930's with the completed book and it was his
pleasure to simply prepare it for publication. But, who
was this mysterious A. J. Russell?

Well, I've gone back and investigated the mysterious
Mr. A. J. Russell and uncovered some shocking facts.
First, I discovered that Russell was a *London Times* newspaper reporter. A devoted disciple of Frank Buchman,
founder of the Oxford Group (later called Moral Rearma-
ment), Russell wrote a book, *For Sinners Only*, that held
Buchman up as a hero and a spiritual giant.

However, Buchman, rumored to be a homosexual, and
his groups came into disrepute and were discredited a few
years later in the late 1930's after the world's press,
including *Time* and *Newsweek* magazines, reported on a
speech in which Buchman praised Adolph Hitler and the
Nazis for their campaign against the Jews in Germany.
Said Buchman, "I thank God for Adolf Hitler." It was also
revealed that Buchman had traveled to Germany on a
secret mission to meet with Heinrich Himmler, head of
the Nazi concentration camps and joint architect of
Hitler's grandiose scheme for a One World Religion
(Societas Satana) planned once the predicted Nazi world
conquest had succeeded.

Buchman's Oxford Group was not exclusively Christian. One could be a Hindu, a Moslem, or a Buddhist and
be a member. Indeed, Buchman is known to have traveled
to India where it is believed he conspired with Hindu
initiates of The Order and worked to set up chapters of
the Oxford Group.

In the Oxford Group itself there were no churches
and no pastors. All that was required was that the
individual sit or kneel quietly each day with pen and paper

in hand and write down impressions and instructions from "God," whomever that was for the individual. This was called Quiet Time and it was during their Quiet Time, Russell alleges, that the two anonymous women authors of *God Calling* received their daily messages from "God."

Evidently, it wasn't "God" alone who always visited Buchman's disciples. Word began to spread that members of the various Oxford Group chapters that had sprung up in Britain, the United States, and elsewhere were getting together for Quiet Time "Spook Parties" and that bizarre spirits from beyond made their presence known. Guidance from these spirits was certainly unorthodox and rumors began to be heard that some groups were involved in sexual misconduct.

In his book, *For Sinners Only*, A. J. Russell reveals experiences with spirit beings whom he could not identify. These spirit beings, he admits, told him what to write and how and where to get his writings published. In one instance, Russell describes a demonic force that attacked and entered him while he lay helplessly paralyzed on his bed.

The Authority of the Holy Bible

Even given this grim history of its editor and the book's coauthors, one might legitimately ask, how can we know for sure that *God Calling* and the many other false "Bibles" and guides are of the devil? Thanks be to God He has given us His Holy Bible as an evaluation tool.

First we see that Jude encourages us to "contend for the faith once delivered to the Saints" (Jude verse 3). How many times delivered? *Once.* So we already have the perfect, definitive guide for our lives--the 100 percent inerrant, wonderful Word of God, from Genesis to Revelation!

Praise Jesus, *we need no other written guide*, for, as Paul warned, there would come a time (I believe it is today) when men "will not endure sound doctrine, but after their own lusts shall they heap to themselves teachers, having itching ears. And they shall turn away their ears from the truth, and shall be turned unto fables" (II Timothy 3:15).

> All scripture is given by inspiration of God, and is profitable for doctrine, for reproof, for correction, for instruction in righteousness: That the man of God may be perfect, throughly furnished unto all good works.
> (II Timothy 3:16-17)

The Heretical Doctrines in God Calling

When we go outside the Bible to other so-called "divinely inspired" books and "Bibles," we are on quicksand. Every one of these false guides is packed with heresy. Every one of them. *God Calling* is no exception. Let me illustrate by pointing out just a few of the many atrocious and ungodly passages from *God Calling*:

(1) Can God be "breathed in" by a person? This is what the Hindus and New Agers teach. They even have deep breathing exercises so an individual can breath in the "universal energy source" said to be "God." This is also exactly what *God Calling* teaches:

> Faith is the soul's breathing in of the Divine Spirit.
> (August 17 devotional.)

Worse yet, whereas the Bible instructs us that the Holy Spirit--Christ within a believer--brings power, *God Calling* states that power comes by our *breathing* it in and that God *cannot* deny us this power:

All Power is given unto Me ... but even I have to acknowledge that I cannot withhold it from the soul that dwells near me .... It is breathed in by the soul who lives in my presence.

(2) According to the Holy Bible, God has sent us the comforter, the Holy Spirit, to lead and guide us. But the New Age and the occult believe that "God" is simply a "Divine Force." *God Calling* also acknowledges this Force, rather than the Holy Spirit:

The Divine Force is sufficient for all the work in the world.

(3) The New Age occult doctrine claims a pantheistic God: "God" is said to be synonymous with "nature." Thus, the earth is divine, the stars and planets are "God," and man is himself "God." All is one. All is "God." Thus, earth is known as Mother Earth, a living, breathing goddess!

God Calling agrees with this New Age heresy, stating that the living Mother Earth is holy and that nature is divine: "She" is even called a "saint:"

Nature is the embodied Spirit of my thoughts .... Treat her as such ... as truly my servant and messenger, as any saint who has ever lived ... (March 8 devotional.)

Earth gave me her best--a human temple to enclose My Divinity, and I brought her the possession of Divine Power, Divine Love, Divine Strength" (August 19 devotional.)

(4) The New Age and occult teach that every man from birth automatically has *God within*, whereas the Bible instructs us that only after a person accepts Jesus Christ as his Lord and Savior does the Holy Spirit enter within. *God Calling* goes along with the New Age doctrine:

Wherever the soul is I am. Man has rarely understood this. I am actually at the centre of every man's being...." (March 26 devotional.)

(5) *God Calling*, in contrast to the Bible, denies that a believer must accept Jesus as Lord and be born again (see John 3:3). Instead, according to *God Calling*, all that's necessary is that the person be conscious that "God" is already present within, then union (a Hindu concept) can occur:

Union with Me may be the result of just consciousness of My Presence. (April 23 devotional.)

(6) New Age and occult religion is based on communication with demon spirits. In contrast, the Bible calls communication with the spirit world an abomination to the Lord (see Deuteronomy 18). *God Calling* falls in the New Age and occult camp by clearly calling on readers to make contact and keep company with spirits from the dead.   For example, we find this declaration in *God Calling: "Trust in the Spirit Forces of the unseen, not in those you see..."*
The devotional of September 6 also encourages us to communicate with the dead in the "Unseen World:"

How often mortals rush to earthly friends who can serve them in so limited a way, when the friends who are freed from the limitations of humanity can serve them so much better, understand better, protect better, plan better, and even plead better their cause with Me.

You do well to remember your friends in the unseen. Companying with them the more you live in this Unseen World, the gentler will be your passing when it comes.

And More Heresies . . .

This is only a sampling of the many false teachings found throughout *God Calling*. Contrary to the Holy Bible, this unholy book also teaches that it is our works that get us into heaven, that we can become wealthy through a "name it and claim it' gospel, that we are to consider God as "business manager and owner" whom we go to with our demands, that man is himself divine and has "God" inside of him, that initiation is required of the believer rather than regeneration, that man's ultimate goal is to attain material things, that we should not wait upon God for our needs but instead "walk into . . . and take," that God resides in a place called the "Spirit World," and that Jesus' return depends not on God's timetable but upon the actions of mankind.

Finally, *God Calling* instructs the reader to forget Bible doctrine and theology, just know *him*, the demon spirit who is the author of *God Calling:* "Know no theology. Know me . . . all you need to know about God you know in me." (November 20 devotional.)

But Jesus cannot be separated from His Word. He is revealed to us by the Bible. This is why Paul told us to "preach the Word, be instant in season and out of season; reprove, rebuke, exhort with all longsuffering and doctrine" (II Timothy 4:2).

Who's Behind God Calling?

The devil well knows that if he can separate us from God's Word, the one and only true Bible, we will fall prey to every wind of doctrine--even to the doctrines of demons. This is why Christians must shy away from embracing the New Age "Bibles" and "scriptures" that Satan's minions are putting out at such a rapid clip today. The Holy Spirit bears witness that our inspiration is to come only from keeping in our hearts *God's established Word:*

I will not forget thy Word (Psalm 119:16).

Thy Word is a lamp unto my feet and a light unto my path (Psalm 119:105).

Forever, O Lord, thy Word is settled in heaven (Psalm 119:;89).

But the Word of the Lord endureth forever. And this is the Word which by the gospel is preached unto you. (I Peter 1:25).

PART FIVE

Starry, Starry Nights . . . Bright New Day

SIXTEEN

What to Do Until the Millennium Comes

*These shall make war with the Lamb, and the Lamb
shall overcome them: for He is Lord of lords, and
King of kings: and they that are with him are called,
and chosen, and faithful.*

(Revelation 17:14)

We are entering an incredible *Seventh
Millennium* of man on planet earth. What
is in *your* immediate future? What lies
just ahead for *your* loved ones? The 1990s are the threshold to what appears to be two dramatic possibilities for
humankind. On the one hand it is conceivable that God,
in His own Wisdom and timing, will decide to end the age
and to usher in His own glorious one thousand-year
millennial reign. On the other hand, we are being offered
quite a different millennium by the powers that be.

If we are to believe our politicians, the international
propagandists, and the economists, we are now entering
the most promising decade in the annals of human history.
They say that this is to be an era of unparalleled peace,
wealth, and tranquility. Seemingly, a way has been found
to insure perpetual prosperity, harmony and love between
all men. A universal religion and a one world political/

economic order are to be the vehicles sure to send us radiantly smiling and euphorically blissful into the glorious, man-made Seventh Millennium.

As I write this book, economies are booming, money is flowing, communist regimes are in disarray everywhere, and democracy is on the rise. Some even predict a One World Democratic Order. Peace seems to be breaking out all over. Interest in religion is at an all-time high. Politicians promise the best is yet to come. *What could possibly go wrong?*

In the book of Daniel, we find that there are certain prophetic events that are *determined* (Daniel 11:36). In other words, they will occur in God's timing and there is absolutely nothing man can do to hurry them up or prevent them. If we are truly to understand the age in which we live, and conduct ourselves honorably while living joyously each day, we need to be aware of these prophetic events which are forecasted by God's Word. We should, therefore, believe God and not man.

While world leaders promise us a sparkling 1990s and a shining, pleasure-filled future, the awful truth is far different. I believe the very foundations of our democratic institutions have begun to crack and crumble. Immorality and a loss of faith in God prove our civilization to be in precariously dangerous circumstances. A strange new world, a remarkable new vista is beckoning mankind into murky and uncharted waters. In *Millennium* I have attempted to navigate those waters using Bible prophecy and the inner guidance of the Holy Spirit as my navigational tools.

When we survey the world about us, and consider the staggering events that are ocurring as well as the ominous landscape that has been prepared for us by the Adversary, our minds virtually go numb. It is undeniable that a plot exists so grave and hideous it should cause Christians everywhere to shake their heads in sadness. If it were not for the grace of God, none of us could face the perilous times ahead without suffering extreme fear and anxiety.

For 6,000 years Satan and an unredeemed, rebellious humanity have jointly conspired against God. *But this rebellion is now in its last stages.* The beast is about to be released from the catacombs, and he will amble his way recklessly toward his ultimate destiny as he journeys to Jerusalem. The dark storm clouds have gathered, now comes the deluge. Yet, rest assured it will all be followed by a *bright new day.*

The Order and its Lords of Money are motivated by money. Yes, the love of money *is* the root of all evil. Any true Christian knows that our hope is not in gold and silver. Not surprisingly, James told us that *in the last days* rich men would "weep and howl" for the miseries that come upon them. Their riches, he prophesied, would be corrupted, their gold and silver tainted. Prophesied James "Ye have heaped treasure together for the last days" (James 5:3).

The question, then, arises: In *what* or *whom* can we place our hope? The magnificent answer: in Jesus Christ. He alone is the blessed hope of believers (I Thessalonians 4:13-18).

I am not at all dismayed about the coming hard times. Forces that oppose goodness and righteousness desire us to fear them. But that is not the way of Christians. Nothing can separate us from the love of Christ. Paul said it best as he outlined all of the things that the Adversary sends our way, hoping to dissuade us and keep us from our appointed tasks in bringing the Great Commission to the world. He says that:

> ... neither death, nor life, nor angels, nor principalities, nor powers, nor things present, nor things to come, nor height, nor depth, nor any other creature, shall be able to separate us from the love of God, which is in Christ Jesus our Lord. (Romans 8:38-39)

God will always stand by His children. Once the elitists have their way and the country plunges headlong into the valley of economic fear, despair, and misery, then moral and spiritual stamina will be required of each of us. In the Great Depression of the 30s, those who were part of strong family units and retained their faith in God prospered spiritually, and were even fortified. For those who have families, I pray that you will strengthen your families and together work joyously as we approach that fantastic day when Jesus Christ comes again.

If perchance you do not have a family by inheritance that you can cling to, whose members you can count on and trust, always remember that *all of us who know Christ Jesus as Lord are in the same family.* I am your brother, and you have many more brothers and sisters as well. But more important, you have a heavenly Father who loves you dearly--and died on the cross *just for you* to prove His love.

Our heavenly Father promised us He would come again and receive us to Himself. Could Jesus Christ Himself come again this decade? I believe with all my heart that this wonderful and exciting possibility exists. True, mortal man cannot know the day nor the hour; yet the Lord Himself advised us to "watch," for "when ye shall see all these things know that it is near, even at the doors" (Matthew 24:13, 33).

In *Millennium,* my fervently desired goal has been to encourage readers to be watchful and to develop a hopeful expectation of His soon return. Though there be cloudy and dark days ahead and even lightnings, thunders, rain, and stormy weather, I am not at all downcast. Every morning when I look in the mirror, I can smile. You see, some years ago I was chosen to live and reign with God in His coming millennium on planet earth. How about you? Will you be there with me in that era when peace and prosperity are guaranteed? Will you be there after the promises of men are proven fruitless and those of God come fully into reality? Will you be side-by-side with me and thousands of others as we sing a song of victory, joyous in the knowledge that all the kingdoms of earth have finally and forevermore become His? If you want Jesus Christ to cleanse and make you whole, if you are willing to commit your life, heart and soul to Him, I pray you will call on Him today. If you will, I promise--He will answer.

And in the days of these kings shall the God of Heaven set up a kingdom, which shall never be destroyed: and the kingdom shall not be lost to other people, but it shall break in pieces and consume all these kingdoms, and it shall stand forever.

(Daniel 2:44)

FOOTNOTES AND REFERENCES

Chapter 1: The Day They Take Our Money Away

1. Jose Arguelles, interviewed by John-Alexis Viereck, *Meditation*, Summer 1987, Vol. II, No. 3, pp. 6-19. And see *Magical Blend*, Issue 18, 1988, pp. 17-20.
2. See Manley P. Hall, *Lectures on Ancient Philosophy*, p. 433, also see the outstanding book *The New World Order*, by Ralph Epperson, (Tucson, Arizona: Publius Press, 1990). This book by Ralph Epperson may be ordered by writing to Publius Press, 3100 South Philamena Place, Tucson, Arizona 85730.
3. Michael Howard, *The Occult Conspiracy: Secret Societies--Their Influence and Power In World History* (New York, New York: Destiny Books, distributed by Harper & Row Publishers, 1989), p. 162.
4. *Ibid.*, p. 163.
5. A. K. Chesterson, *The New Unhappy Lords*, 3rd American edition, January 1970, (reprinted 1979), p. 197.
6. *Ibid.*, p. 1.
7. Senator Jesse Helms, quoted in *Flashpoint*, January 1990, p. 2.
8. Alice Bailey, *From Bethlehem to Calvary* (New York: Lucis Publishing Company, 1965), p. 30.
9. Jose Arguelles, *Whole Life Times*, Issue No. 3, 1987.
10. Gaetan Delaforge, *The Templar Tradition And The Age of Aquarius*
11. *Gnosis*, Winter 1990.
12. LaVedi Lafferty and Bud Hollowell, *Eternal Dance* (St. Paul, Minnesota: Llewelyn Publications, 1983), p. 468.
13. Alice Bailey, *Discipleship in The New Age*, Vol. II (New York: Lucis Trust, 1955), p. 102. And see the pamphlet, *The New Group of World Servers*, World Goodwill, New York, New York.
14. *Building and Bridging: The New Group of World Servers*, published by School for Esoteric Studies, New York, New York.
15. Omraam Aizanhov, *Aquarius: Hero of The Golden Age*, (Part 1) Vol. 25, (Prosvet S.A., 1981), p. 232.
16. Randall N. Baer, *Inside the New Age Nightmare*, (Lafayette, Louisiana: Huntington House, Inc., 1989), pp. 92-93.

Chapter 2: Secret Societies and Other Conspiracies

1. Marilyn Ferguson, *The Aquarian Conspiracy* (Los Angeles, California: J. P. Tarcher, Inc., 1980).
2. Eklal Kueshana, *The Ultimate Frontier* (Quinlan, Texas: The Stelle Group, 1963), p. 7.
3. *Ibid.*, p. 140.
4. *Network News*, published by the Tara Center, Vol. VII, No. 7-8, July-August, 1990, p. 1.
5. Alice Bailey, *Discipleship in the New Age*, Vol. II (New York: Lucis Publishing Company, seventh printing, 1986, third edition).
6. John Randolph Price, *Practical Spirituality* (Austin, Texas: Quartus Books, 1985), p. 122.

7. Vera Stanley Alder, *The Initiation Of The World* (York Beach, Maine: Samuel Weiser, Inc., 1972).
8. Djwhal Khul, see Alice Bailey, *Esoteric Psychology II* (New York: Lucis Trust Publishing, 1970), p. 282. Also see Sir John Sinclair, *The Alice Bailey Inheritance* (Wellingborough, Northamptonshire: Turnstone Press Limited, 1984), p. 124.
9. J. R. Church, *Guardians of the Grail* (Oklahoma City, Oklahoma: Prophecy Publications, 1989).
10. "Europe's Hidden King," *Harper and Queen*, March, 1990.
11. U.S. Senator Barry Goldwater, *With No Apologies* (quoted in *The Omega Letter*, February, 1989), p. 8.
12. *Ibid.*
13. *Ibid.*
14. *Ibid.*
15. *Ibid.*
16. Francois Hervet, "Knights of Darkness: the Sovereign Military Order of Malta," *Covert Action*, No. 25 (Winter 1986), pp. 27-38. Also see James Mann with Kathleen Phillips, "Inside Look at Those Elite Religious Groups," *US News and World Report*, March 19, 1989, pp. 60-61.
17. Hervet, *Ibid.*
18. Steven M. L. Aronson, "George Bush's Biggest Secret," *Fame*, August, 1989, pp. 82-89.
19. *Ibid.*
20. *Ibid.*
21. For example, see the thought-provoking book *In God's Name*, by David Yallop and the revealing book *Christianity and American Freemasonry*, by William J. Whalen.

Chapter 3: **When the Light Hits, the Dark Gets Tough**

1. Alice Bailey, *The Externalization of the Hierarchy* (New York, NY: Lucis Trust) p. 511.
2. *Ibid.*, p. 569.
3. *Ibid.*, p. 574.
4. *Ibid.*, p. 58.
5. Jose Arguelles, interviewed by John-Alexis Viereck, *Meditation* magazine, Summer, 1987, pp. 6-19. Also see Antero Alli, "A Post-Convergence Interview with Jose Arguelles," *Magical Blend* magazine, issue 18, 1988, pp. 17-20.
6. Quoted by Antero Alli, *Ibid.*, p. 18.
7. *Ibid.*
8. *Share International News*, Volume 1, Number 1, 1990.
9. "The Coming Stockmarket Crash," *Share International*, Volume 8, Number 4, May, 1989.
10. Richard Lamm, "U.S. Will Pay for its Excesses," *The Republic*, January 24, 1990. Also, see Lamm's book, *Megatraumas: America in the Year 2000.*
11. Benjamin Creme, "The Coming Stock Market Crash," *Share International*, Volume 8, Number 4, May 1989.
12. Alice A. Bailey, *Esoteric Psychology* (Volume 2) (New York, NY: Lucis Publishing Company, 1970/Eighth printing, 1981), p. 730-731.
13. *Ibid.*
14. *Ibid.*

15. Joseph E. Slater, *Free Man's Digest*, January, 1979, p. 24.
16. Joseph Slater, see *Free Man's Digest*, January, 1979, p. 28, and *Free Man's Digest*, January, 1979.
17. Aurelio Peccei, quoted in the *Calgary Albertan*, "Club of Rome Says Messiah is Needed," April 18, 1980.
18. *Ibid.*
19. Ravi Batra, *The Great Depression of 1990*, (Baal Publishing: 1987) p. 35.
20. *Ibid.*
21. Thomas Ehrenzeller, *Solar Man* (Winona, Minnesota: Apollo Books, 1985).
22. Christopher Hyatt, quoted in "Undoing Yourself," by Antero Alli, *Magical Blend* magazine, Issue No. 16, 1987, p. 22.
23. Ruth Montgomery, *Threshold to Tomorrow* (New York, NY: Fawcett Press, 1982), pp. 206-207.
24. *Ibid.*
25. See Texe Marrs, *Mystery Mark of the New Age*, p. 153; and see Alice Bailey, "Food for Thought," *Whole Life Times* magazine, Winter, 1986-87, p. 57 and pp. 71-72.
26. Thomas P. Ehrenzeller, *Solar Man*, pp. 244-247.

Chapter 4: **The Order and Its Master Plan**

1. Benjamin Creme, *Share International*, Vol. 8, No. 3, April, 1989, p. 2.
2. Vera Stanley Alder, *When Humanity Comes of Age* (New York, New York: Samuel Weiser, Inc., 1974) p. 190-193.
3. John Randolph Price, *The Planetary Commission* (Austin, Texas: Quartus Books, 1984) pp. 47-48.
4. Robert Muller, *New Genesis: Shaping a Global Spirituality* (New York, New York, Doubleday: 1984), p. 29.
5. Jack Bolin, "The Master Mind Principle," *Master Mind Goal Achievers Journal* (Warren, Michigan: Master Mind Publishing Company, 1985), p. 2. Also see Texe Marrs, *Mystery Mark of The New Age* (Westchester, Illinois: Crossway Books, 1987).
6. Thomas Ehrenzeller, *Solar Man*.
7. *Ibid.*, p. 3.
8. *Ibid.*, p. 5.
9. *Ibid.*, p. 6.
10. *Ibid.*, p. 51.
11. *Ibid.*, p. 54.
12. *Ibid.*, p. 56.
13. *Ibid.*, p. 57.
14. *Ibid.*, p. 179.
15. Joshua Halpern, *Children of the Dawn: Vision of the New Family*, (Bodega, California: Only With Love Publications, 1986), p. 183.
16. Foster Bailey, *Running God's Plan* (New York, NY: Lucis Trust), p. 53.
17. C. Brent Bergsten, quoted in the *Christian Science Monitor*, August 9, 1989.
18. *Wall Street Journal*, November 19, 1982, and see Texe Marrs, *Mega Forces*, (Austin, Texas: Living Truth Publishers, 1988) pp. 212, 213.
19. Marrs, *Ibid.*, p. 213.

Chapter 5: A World Leader for the New Millennium

1. Alice Bailey, *op.cit.*
2. Vera Stanley Alder, *When Humanity Comes Of Age* (New York: Samuel Weiser, Inc., 1974) pp. 45-49.
3. *Ibid.*, p. 173.
4. *Ibid.*
5. *Ibid.*
6. *Ibid.*
7. See Russell Braddon, *Japan Against The World: 1941-2041: The One Hundred Year War For Supremacy* (New York, New York: Stein and Day, 1983).
8. *The Testament of Adolf Hitler: The Hitler-Borman Documents*, February-April 1945, p. iv.
9. Aleister Crowley, quoted by Robert Anton Wilson in *Cosmic Trigger: Final Secrets of The Illuminati* (Phoenix, Arizona: Falcon Press, 1986).
10. Henry C. Clausen, 33rd degree, *Emergence of The Mystical* (2nd edition) (Washington, D.C.: The Supreme Council of the Ancient and Accepted Scottish Rite of Freemasonry of the Southern Jurisdiction of the United States of America), p. 18.

Chapter 6: Occult Theocracy

1. See *Insight* magazine, July 3, 1989 and *Prophecy in the News*, October, 1988, p. 4.
2. See Dana Ullman, "Royal Medicine," *New Age Journal*, September/October 1987, pp. 45-52, 62; and the book, *The Prince and the Paranormal* (London: W. H. Allen and Company).
3. "Prince Urges Debt Bargain," *Sunday Mail*, Adelaide, Australia, October 29, 1989.
4. See Larry Abraham, "Global Land Grab," *Conservative Digest*, September 1988, pp. 61-66. Also see footnote above--*Sunday Mail*.
5. Stephen Kinzer, *New York Times*, June 20, 1987.
6. *The Sunday Oregonian*, January 3, 1988, p. B3, orginally reported in *The Washington Post*.
7. *Ibid.*
8. *Ibid.*
9. *Washington Post*, page C4, February 18, 1986.
10. *Human Events*, July, 1983, p. 18.
11. *World Goodwill Newsletter*, No. 3, 1990, p. 1.
12. David Ellis, "Gorby: The New Age Guru?," *Time* magazine, May 18, 1990.
13. See Texe Marrs, "Gorbachev: The World's Top New Age Leader?," *Flashpoint* newsletter, September 1990.
14. Mikhail Gorbachev, *Perestroika: New Thinking For Our Country and the World* (New York, New York: Harper & Row, 1987), pp. 144-145.
15. *Ibid.*
16. *Ibid.*, p. 29.
17. *Ibid.*, p. 50.
18. *Ibid.*, p. 137.
19. See Gorbachev's book, *Toward a Better World*, 1987.
20. *Ibid.*, p. 231.
21. *New Frontier*, November, 1987.

Chapter 7: When Will The Dollar Die?

1. Michael Claudon, editor, *World Debt Crisis: International Lending On Trial* (Cambridge, Massachusetts: Ballinger Publishing Company, 1986), p. xix.
2. John Zajac, *Delicate Balance: Coming Catastrophic Changes on Planet Earth* (Lafayette, Louisiana: Huntington House, Inc., 1989), p. 62, 63.
3. *Ibid.*
4. Ron Paul, quoted in *The Coming Currency Exchange* (Oklahoma City, Oklahoma: Southwest Radio Church, 1984), p. 23.
5. *Ibid.*, p. 2.
6. *Ibid.*, p. 8.
7. *Ibid.*
8. "The Coloring of Greenbacks," *The Washington Post*, quoted in *The Coming Currency Exchange*.
9. Emmanuel Swedenbourg, "Funny Money," *The Clairvoyant*, Vol. II, No. 1, p. 18.
10. Bill Baxter, quoted in *The Coming One World Currency*, by Salem Kirban (Huntingdon Valley, Pennsylvania: Second Coming, Inc., 1989), pp. 13, 14.
11. *Ibid.*
12. Ingo Walter, *The Secret Money Market* (New York: Harper & Row, Publishers).
13. William Raspberry, "Root of All Evil," *The Washington Post*, reprinted in *The Austin American Statesman*, July 7, 1989, p. A14.
14. *Ibid.*
15. *Ibid.*
16. "Former Treasury Secretary Wants Currency Exchange," *Daily Oklahoman*, September 19, 1989 (originally published in the *New York Times*).
17. Nicholas Brady, quoted in article "Battle to Reduce US Dollar's Value Brings War at Home," *Austin American Statesman*, October 8, 1989, p. H5.
18. Ron Paul, *op. cit*, p. 5.
19. *Ibid.*, p. 6.

Chapter 8: Signs of Impending Disaster

1. "S&L Losses Pile Up Despite Bailout," (Associated Press, for example see *Austin American Statesman*, December 22, 1989, p. 8).
2. *USA Today*, March 27, 1990, pp. 1B-2B.
3. Jim McTague and Mindy Fetergman, "Bad Loans, Competition Take Their Toll," *USA Today*, May 29, 1990, pp. B1-B2.
4. *Ibid.*, also see Gary North: Special Report, "The Upheaval of the 90s and Your Money."
5. Salem Kirban, *The Coming One World Currency* (Huntingdon Valley, Pennsylvania: Second Coming, Inc., 1989), pp. 19-22.
6. *Business Week*, July 16, 1990, p. 178.
7. *New York Times*, June 7, 1987.
8. Ron Paul, *op. cit.*, p. 123.
9. "Summit," *Houston Chronicle*, Sunday, July 29, 1990, p. 4E.

10. Lenin, quoted by Gary Allan, *None Dare Call it Conspiracy* (Concord Press, 1971), pp. 41-42.
11. See *The McAlvaney Intelligence Advisor*, January, 1990, p. 5.
12. Quoted by Micheline Maynard, "Auto Sales Plunge in Early August," *USA Today*, August 15, 1990, p. B1.
13. "Food--the Essential Commodity," *Countdown*, Vol. 1, No. 2, April 1990, pp. 5, 20.
14. Robert Baker, "Collapse in Food Stocks Reduces Aid," *The New Federalist*, December 1, 1989, p. 1.
15. Robert Pear, "Bush to Call for Drop in Deficit," *The New York Times.* And see *The Kansas City Times*, January 27, 1990, p. 1.

Chapter 9: The Coming Collapse of The Money System

1. Norman A. Bailey, "The World Economy in the 1990s," *The World And I,* January 1990, pp. 30-41.
2. *Ibid.*, p. 33
3. *Ibid.*, p. 34
4. *Ibid.*
5. *Ibid.*, p. 33
6. *Ibid.*, p. 36
7. *Ibid.*, p.33
8. Howard Wachtel, quoted by Clyde H. Farnsworth, "Global Crunch: Can Nations Set Aside Their Parochialism In Time?," *New York Times*, November 1, 1987, section 4, p. 1.
9. Ron Paul, *op. cit.*, pp. 22, 23.
10. John Zajac, *Delicate Balance: Coming Catastrophic Changes on Planet Earth*, p. 65.
11. *Ibid.*
12. *Ibid.*
13. William Greider, quoted by Deborah Baldwin, "Invasion of the Fed Watchers," *Common Cause*, March/April 1988, pp. 26-32.
14. Abner Arbel and Albert E. Kaff, *Crash: Ten Days in October...Will it Strike Again?* (Illinois: Longman Financial Services Publishing, 1989).
15. Robert W. Faid, *Gorbachev! Has the Real Antichrist Come?* (Tulsa, Oklahoma: Victory House Publishers, 1988).
16. Quoted in "Wall Street's Agony: A View From Afar," *The New York Times*, Sunday, November 1, 1987, p. E3.
17. *Ibid.*
18. *Ibid.*

Chapter 10: The Looting of America

1. Mark Memmott, "U.S. Debt up 25 Percent to $664 Billion," *USA Today*, July 3, 1990, p. B1.
2. Paul Blustein, "Weaving a Web of Fiscal Deceit," Washington Post Service, (*Austin American Statesman*), February 4, 1990, p. C1.
3. "Will Foreigners Shape Bush Policies?" *Wall Street Journal*, December 5, 1988, p. 1.
4. Thomas Olmstead, "Selling Off America," *Foreign Policy*, Fall 1989, pp. 119-140.

5. John Hillkirk, "USA Selling off our Real Wealth," *USA Today*, July 28, 1988, p. 1. (Also see, Olmstead, Ibid., p. 120.)
6. Olmstead, *op. cit.*, p. 121.
7. Senator Frank Murkowski, quoted in *New York Times*, December 30, 1985.
8. Olmstead, *op. cit.*, p. 126.
9. "The Global 1,000 - The Leaders," *Business Week*, July 16, 1990, pp. 112-142
10. John Hillkirk, "Numbers Stirs Debate on Capital Hill," *USA Today*, July 28, 1988, p. B1.
11. *Ibid.*
12. Martin Mayer, "The Transaction Tax's Evil Twin," *Wall Street Journal*, July 13, 1990, p. A8.
13. "The Next Four Years," *Foreign Affairs*, published by the Council on Foreign Relations (CFR), New York, Winter 1988/1989.
14. *Ibid.*, p. 7.
15. *Ibid.*, p. 17.
16. See John Barela, "The Case of the Vanishing Gold," *Front Page* (A publication of Today, The Bible and You), May 1990. Also see the book *The Federal Reserve Scandal*, by Bill Sampson and Billy James Hargis, and *The Secrets of the Federal Reserve*, by Eustace Mullins.

Chapter 11: **The New International Economic Order**

1. President Ronald Reagan, quoted in *Newswatch*, June 1988, p. 5 and "Reagan Advocates One Worldism," *The Spotlight*, February 1, 1988.
2. World Goodwill, "The Economic Problem: Finance, Trade and the Global Economy," 1987 (Number 3).
3. *The New International Economic Order*, World Goodwill Commentary Number 14, September, 1980.
4. *Ibid.*
5. "The Two Super-powers Forge New World Order," *New York Times*, circa 1989.
6. *Ibid.*, p. 5.
7. *Ibid.*, p. 4.
8. *Ibid.*, p. 24.
9. *The Economist*, January 9, 1988.
10. *Ibid.*
11. See Barbara Walker, *The Women's Encyclopedia of Myths and Secrets*, (San Francisco, California: Harper and Row Publishers, 1983), p. 798.
12. *Ibid.*
13. *Newswatch*, September, 1986.
14. *Multinational Monitor*, January 1982.

Chapter 12: **The New Rome and the Resurrection of Hitler's Ghost**

1. Quoted by L. Craig Frasier, *The Testament of Adolf Hitler: The Hitler-Borman Documents.*
2. *Ibid.*
3. See Constance Cumbey, *The Hidden Dangers of The Rainbow*, (Lafayette, Louisiana: Huntington House Publishers, 1983).

4. Benjamin Creme, *Maitreya's Mission*, (North Hollywood, California: Share International), p. 209.
5. *Ibid.*
6. See Robert Anton Wilson, *Cosmic Trigger: Final Secret of The Illuminati*, pp. 109-110.
7. *Ibid.*, p. 110.
8. A. Tyne, *New York Times*, circa 1990.
9. Cumbey, *op. cit.*
10. Benjamin Creme, *op. cit.*
11. *Chicago Tribune*, July 2, 1922.

Chapter 13: Babylon Comes Alive!--Lighting Up the Fiery Furnaces Once Again

1. Joseph Chambers, *The End Times and Victorious Living*, Vol. 4, No. 4, May 1990, p. 1.
2. *Ibid.*
3. Joseph Chambers, *Babylon Rises Again* (Oklahoma City, Oklahoma: Southwest Radio Church, 1990), pp. 2-7.
4. See *Time*, June 11, 1990.
5. Vera Stanley Alder, *The Initiation of The World* (New York: Samuel Weiser, Inc., 1972), pp. 115-125, 242.
6. See, for example, the book *From Eden to Eros*, by Richard Roberts (San Anselmo, California: Vernal Equinox Press, 1985), p. 19.

Chapter 14: A Supernatural Faith for the New Millennium

1. Joshua Halpern, *Children of the Dawn: Vision of the New Family*, pp. 24-25.
2. *Ibid.*, p. 183.
3. Vera Stanley Alder, *The Initiation of the World* (New York: Samuel Weiser, Inc., 1976), p. 138.
4. *Ibid.*
5. Kai King, "The New Age," *Gabriel's Horn*, Spring 1988, p. 19.
6. Alice Bailey, *The Labors of Hercules*, 3rd printing (New York, New York: Lucis Publishing Co., 1982), pp. 182-183.
7. Ruth Montgomery, *Aliens Among Us*, pp. 170-171.
8. *Ibid.*, p. 171.
9. John Randolph Price, *The Planetary Commission* (Austin, Texas: Quartus Books, 1984), p. 29.
10. *Ibid.*, pp. 47-48.
11. *Ibid.*, p. 165.
12. *Ibid.*, p. 166.
13. *Ibid.*, p. 171.
14. *Ibid.*, p. 163.
15. Alice Bailey, *The Rays and The Initiations* (New York, New York: Lucis Trust Publishing Co., 1982), p. 50.
16. *Ibid.*, p. 95.
17. As quoted by Texe Marrs in *Dark Secrets of the New Age* (Westchester, Illinois: Good News Publishers, 1987), p. 89.
18. Alice Bailey, *The Rays and the Initiations*, *op. cit.*, p. 94.

19. Benjamin Creme, *Maitreya's Mission* (Amsterdam: Share International Foundation), p. 160.
20. Benjamin Creme, *Messages From Maitreya the Christ* (Amsterdam: Share International), p. 22.
21. *Ibid.*, p. 202.
22. Benjamin Creme, *Maitreya's Mission*, *op. cit.*, p. 128.
23. *Ibid.*, pp. 316-319.
24. Benjamin Creme, *Messages From Maitreya the Christ*, *op. cit.*, p. 178.
25. *Ibid.*, p. 325.
26. Alice Bailey, *Ponder on This*, (New York, New York: Lucis Publishing), p. 283.
27. David Spangler, *Revelation: the Birth of a New Age* (Middleton, Wisconsin: Lorian Press, 1976), p. 24.
28. Laeh Garfield, *Companions in Spirit* (Berkely, California: Celestial Arts, 1984).
29. Barry McWaters, *Conscious Evolution: Personal and Planetary Evolution*, (San Francisco, California: Evolutionary Press, 1982), pp. 113-114; and see p. 15.
30. John Randolph Price, *The Superbeings* (Austin, Texas: Quartus Books, 1981), pp. 3, 37-38, 51-52.
31. Foster Bailey, *Running God's Plan* (New York: Lucis Publishing, 1974), p. 11.
32. Alice Bailey, *Ponder on This*, pp. 400-404.
33. *Ibid.*, p. 404.

Chapter 15: Possession is Nine-tenths of the Law

1. Jose Arguelles, "Harmonic Convergence Trigger Event: Implementation and Follow-up," *Whole Life Times*, Volume 1, Number 3, pp. 6i3-65.
2. *Ibid.*
3. Benjamin Creme, *The Reappearancae of the Christ and The Masters of Wisdom* (London: The Tara Press, 1980), p. 59.
4. Alice Bailey, *Ponder on This*, p. 722.
5. *Ibid.*, p. 283.
6. David Spangler, *Revelation: Birth of a New Age*, p. 24.
7. Lyn Andrews, *Meditation*, Summer, 1988, pp. 18-19.
8. Robert Leichtman, M.D. and Carl Japikse, *Magical Blend*, Feb-Apr 88, p. 38.
9. *Ibid.*
10. *Ibid.*, p. 38, 39.
11. *God Calling*, edited by A. J. Russell, many publishers.

About the Author

Well-known author of the #1 national Christian bestseller, *Dark Secrets of The New Age*, **Texe Marrs** has also written 20 other books for such major publishers as Simon & Schuster, John Wiley, Prentice Hall/Arco, Stein & Day, and Dow Jones-Irwin. His books have sold over 700,000 copies.

Texe Marrs was assistant professor of aerospace studies, teaching American defense policy, strategic weapons systems, and related subjects at the University of Texas at Austin from 1977 to 1982. He has also taught international affairs, political science, and psychology for two other universities. A graduate Summa Cum Laude from Park College, Kansas City, Missouri he earned his Master's degree at North Carolina State University.

As a career USAF officer (now retired), he commanded communications-electronics and engineering units. He holds a number of military decorations including the Vietnam Service Medal, and served in Germany, Italy, and throughout Asia.

President of Living Truth Ministries in Austin, Texas, Texe Marrs is a frequent guest on radio and TV talk shows throughout the U.S.A. and Canada in response to the public's search for greater insight into Bible prophecy, world events, the New Age Movement, and the many challenges to Christianity. He addresses these issues head-on in his latest books, *Mystery Mark of The New Age*, and *Ravaged by the New Age*. His monthly newsletter, *Flashpoint*, is distributed around the world.

For Our Newsletter

Texe Marrs offers a free newsletter about Bible prophecy and world events, the New Age Movement, cults, and the occult challenge to Christianity.

If you would like to receive this newsletter, please write to:

Living Truth Ministries
8103-P Shiloh Court
Austin, Texas 78745

Also by Texe Marrs--at Bookstores

Books

TEXE MARRS BOOK OF NEW AGE CULTS AND RELIGIONS

RAVAGED BY THE NEW AGE: Satan's Plan to Destroy Our Kids

MYSTERY MARK OF THE NEW AGE: Satan's Design for World Domination

DARK SECRETS OF THE NEW AGE: Satan's Plan for a One World Religion

MEGA FORCES: Signs and Wonders of the Coming Chaos

Videos

TEXE MARRS EXPOSES SATAN'S NEW AGE PLAN FOR A ONE WORLD ORDER: Is the Reign of the Antichrist Just Ahead?

Tapes

NIGHT COMETH! The New Age Beast and His Riders of Death

NIGHTSOUNDS: The Hidden Dangers of New Age Music